CW00323422

THE · MACDON

Roses

THE · MACDONALD · ENCYCLOPEDIA · OF

Roses

Stelvio Coggiatti

Macdonald Orbis

ACKNOWLEDGEMENT

The Publisher would like to thank the following for their invaluable assistance: Croix de Bourg Argenteuil, Delbard of Paris, Hauser of Vaumarcus, Kriloff of Antibes, Meilland of Cap d'Antibes (also for the photographs by G. Meunier), Mr R. C. Balfour of the Royal National Rose Society for supplying photographs, and the many personal friends of the author for providing answers to the most taxing problems.

A *Macdonald Orbis* BOOK
© Arnoldo Mondadori Editore S.p.A., Milan 1986
© in the English translation
  Arnoldo Mondadori Editore S.p.A., Milan 1987

Translated by John Gilbert

First published in Great Britain in 1987
by Macdonald & Co (Publishers) Ltd
London & Sydney

A member of BPCC plc

All rights reserved
No part of this publication may be reproduced, stored in a retrieval system, or transmitted, in any form or by any means without the prior permission in writing of the publisher, nor be otherwise circulated in any form of binding or cover other than that in which it is published and without a similar condition including this condition being imposed on the subsequent purchaser.

British Library Cataloguing in Publication Data

Macdonald encyclopedia of roses
  1. Roses — Dictionaries
  635.9'33372'0321   SB411

  ISBN 0-356-14275-2

Printed and bound in Italy
by Officine Grafiche A. Mondadori Editore,
Verona

Macdonald & Co (Publishers) Ltd
Greater London House
Hampstead Road
London NW1 7QX

CONTENTS

EXPLANATION OF SYMBOLS

Bush with large flowers
(not in clusters)

nonrecurrent

recurrent

Bush with clusters of flowers

nonrecurrent

recurrent

Bush with small flowers and Polyanthas

nonrecurrent

recurrent

Shrub

nonrecurrent

recurrent

Ground cover

nonrecurrent

recurrent

Climber

nonrecurrent

recurrent

Rambler

nonrecurrent

recurrent

Climbing sport

nonrecurrent

recurrent

Climber with clusters of flowers

nonrecurrent

recurrent

 Botanical species and/or of historic interest

 Accompanied by one of preceding symbols, indicates Hybrid Tea

Note

We should make it clear that the roses described in this book are "garden roses" – we do not deal with roses normally marketed as cut flowers.

The illustrated section of Plates is subdivided into four parts:

☐ botanical species and first-generation descendants
○ bush and shrub roses up to 1910
△ climbing roses up to 1910
◊ garden roses from 1911 to the present day.

The information contained in each entry concerns the origin, description, and use of the variety shown.

THE ROSE'S REMOTE ORIGINS

Although figures are very approximate, it is believed that the human race has been present on earth for some 400,000 years; yet fossil remains discovered in Japan, the United States, France, Germany and Czechoslovakia suggest that the rose has existed for perhaps ten times longer. Admittedly, none of the fossils so far found bears any impression of petals; but they do show the outlines of complete leaves, individual leaflets and twigs with thorns, identifiable as belonging to the genus *Rosa*.

Most authors agree that roses of prehistoric times, like the botanical roses of the present day, possessed simple flowers, i.e. with five petals. The only rose known to have corollas of four petals is *Rosa sericea*, introduced into Europe from the Himalayas at the end of the nineteenth century. This characteristic was passed on to some of its varieties, including *R. s. pteracantha*, additionally notable for its attractive, large, flat red thorns which, on young branches, are translucent and shiny.

Another interesting fact about the genus *Rosa* concerns its distribution. It is found exclusively in certain zones of the northern hemisphere; there are no roses that grow wild in the southern hemisphere.

Fossil finds testify to the remote origins of the rose; but millions of years went by without any further evidence of its presence. Then, during the excavations carried out by Sir Arthur Evans at Knossos (Crete), site of the famous royal palace of Minos (dating from *c.* 2000 BC), initially damaged by an earthquake and later completely destroyed by fire, fragments were found of rare frescoes depicting naturalistic subjects. Visitors to the Herakleion Museum in Crete, where these remains are kept, cannot fail to be impressed by the powerfully expressive likeness of a bluebird, in the fresco which has been given that name, and of the flowers surrounding it, including lilies, iris, crocuses and, especially, roses. This is the oldest artistic representation of the rose, obviously dating from before the fifteenth century BC, when the devastating fire occurred. The discovery understandably aroused keen interest in botanists and rose growers, who even tried to identify the species depicted, eventually deciding, by process of elimination, that it was either *R. gallica*—i.e. *R. milesia*—or *R. praenestina*, or perhaps the Roman *R. rubra*.*

The anomalous presence on one of the Knossos roses of six petals has authoritatively been ascribed to the personal initiative of the artist who long ago restored the fresco; another theory suggests that this

---

* There is some doubt as to whether this last name was actually used in Roman times; it appears in botanical works of the second half of the eighteenth century (Elizabeth Blackwell's *Herbarium* and Jean Baptiste de Lamarck's *Flore française*). Krüssmann (in *Roses*) mentions St Albertus Magnus, predating the first written testimony to the use of the name *Rosa rubra* to the eleventh century. The botanist Gaspare Bauhin (1550–1624), in his *Pinax*, also lists a large number of roses under the overall title of *Rosa rubra*, including a *Rosa rubra praecox flore semplici exiguo odore*, casting doubts on its relationship to the modern *Rosa gallica*.

Leaf of a fossil rose, dating back about 40 million years.

six-petaled flower represents the first phase in a transition from a single to a double corolla, such a transformation being quite consistent, in any event, with *R. gallica.*

We read in Homer (*Iliad*, XXIII) that Hector's body, before burial, was anointed with balsam of roses; this reference provides sufficient proof that during the Trojan War (1200 BC) enough plants were grown to provide large quantities of petals. The same conclusion can be drawn from excavations which prove the existence, during that same period, of terracotta slabs used as receipts for the purchase of rose oil consigned to the palace of Nestor at Pylos in Peloponnesus.

Five centuries later a poet, generally assumed at that time to be Sappho, coined the happy expression: "If Jove wished to give the flowers a queen, the rose ought to be crowned." And Herodotus of Halicarnassus, the "father of history" (fifth century BC), rather surprisingly noted the presence in the garden of King Midas of "a rose with sixty petals which had a sweeter perfume than any other rose." Attempts to identify this rose have led to the conclusion that this must have been a double variety of *R. gallica.*

The Greek philosopher Theophrastus, one of the earliest botanists, also makes several mentions of roses, for example: "Roses differ greatly from one another in the number of petals, roughness of branches, beauty of color and sweetness of perfume. Many have five petals, others twelve or twenty, and a few even more, notably those known as 'centifolia' [Latin *folia* means both petal and leaf] ... As a rule, the soil influences both their color and their scent; the sweetest-smelling roses are those from Cyrene."

Rosa prænestina variegata.

Dioscorides, the Greek physician of the first century AD who contributed so greatly to the spread of knowledge about natural history with his *Materia Medica*, mentions the refreshing and astringent qualities of rose petals.

There are references to roses in the works of various Roman authors who wrote on agriculture (Varro, Columella, Rutilius Palladius and Gargilius Martialis), but especially in the writings of Pliny the Elder, who devoted a large part of Book XXI of his massive thirty-seven volume *Historia Naturalis* to roses. Pliny describes at least eight varieties, but almost invariably gives them the name of the place where they grow (Campana, Praenestina, Milesia, etc.), so that it is possible that the number of genuine varieties was smaller.

Much caution needs to be exercised in attributing modern botanical names to ancient roses. In fact, experienced Greek and Latin scholars who, over the centuries, have translated agricultural texts have often come up against serious difficulties in identifying plants on the basis of descriptions, frequently very generalized, of ancient authors; and even greater problems in trying to determine species and varieties in accordance with modern classification. Aware of the risks of giving wrong names, the translators have often consulted botanists or agricultural experts; sometimes this team-work has had happy results, but just as frequently there have been conflicting opinions because the agronomist will have based his findings not on the original Greek or Latin text but on a translation.

Even so, we know that the following roses definitely existed in

Roman times: among the single-flowered species, *R. canina*, and among the double-flowered *R. gallica, R.* x *alba,* * *R.* x *damasce-na* (in spite of the name, there is no proof that it came from Damascus) and a so-called *R.* x *centifolia*, which evidently flourished in both forms. Indeed, there is reason to believe that the roses with sixty and one hundred petals mentioned by Herodotus, Theophrastus and Pliny may actually be one or other of the double-flowered varieties of *R. gallica*, but another theory is that they belonged to a group that has since vanished. The name *R.* x *centifolia* reappeared toward the end of the sixteenth century, being applied to what the botanists term a hybrid species, with the addition of the adjective *hollandica* or *batavica*, although there are indications that it also grew at that time in southern France.

During the first half of the seventeenth century there were reports of an interesting anomaly in Holland, England and France: in certain roses the five parts of the calyx (sepals), the receptacle below and part of the stem appeared to be covered with a soft, dense, velvety moss which gave out a strong and individual scent. Interest in these moss roses (with a few exceptions all *centifolia*) set a fashion which persisted until the beginning of the present century and encouraged some rose growers to create a series of new varieties.

After a period of neglect, the recently reawakened interest in

* The mark "x" placed between the generic and specific names indicates hybrid origin (spontaneous or artificial crosses between two species).

Page 12: Rosa praenestina variegata *(from a seventeenth-century Herbal).*

Page 13: *the characteristic shape and "mossing" of the sepals is very pronounced in the buds of* R. centifolia cristata *("Chapeau de Napoléon").*

old roses has included the moss roses, especially those varieties which are very heavily mossed (such as the "Common Moss" or "Communis") and those with a recurrent (repeat-flowering) habit, such as "Salet." "Cristata," better known as "Chapeau de Napoléon," was for over a century included among the moss roses; but this rose is a distinct anomaly, owing to mutation; in this particular case it produces a characteristic crest of fronds on its sepals which, before the buds open, take on a pattern reminiscent of the outline of Napoleon's hat.

In Roman times roses played an important role in everyday life; they were fashioned into wreaths and garlands for guests at meals and festive occasions, they were given as presents to a loved one and they were scattered on tombs, while the petals were used to make the *Patina de rosis* (a rose tart) and also a perfumed wine. Rose oil (*rosatum*) was likewise applied for a number of curative purposes. Roses were also grown in glass-houses *ante litteram* and were sprayed with warm water in order to produce flowers in the winter as well, a practice which aroused the anger of Seneca against "*eos qui naturam invertunt.*"

In the ensuing centuries and up to the late Middle Ages we encounter roses in convents (bearing in mind that these religious houses were also oases of culture and science), although historians and chroniclers have commented little on the subject. In the eighth century Charlemagne published a *Capitulare de villis* in which were listed those plants which deserved to be grown in the royal *horti*; the rose came second, after the lily. During the ninth century the monk Walafridus Strabus (Strabo) composed a poem which praised the beauty of flowers and the rose in particular; and in the thirteenth century Saint Albertus Magnus, today the patron saint of botanists, showed that he was an accurate observer of nature, giving detailed descriptions of various roses, including *R. x alba*.

The first part of the *Roman de la Rose*, an illuminated manuscript dating from the beginning of the thirteenth century, describes the state of mind of a young man who tries to win his loved one in the guise of a rose; the concluding phrase of the poem, in the Latinized French of the day, reads: "*Esplicit le livre de la rose où l'ars d'amor est toute enclose.*"

As time passed, the roses that had grown in Roman gardens produced varieties which aroused a good deal of public interest. Thus *R. gallica officinalis*, probably as a result of natural mutation, produced the first variegated rose (red with white streaks), still grown today under the botanical name of *R. g. versicolor*, though perhaps better known as "Rosa Mundi;" *R. g. officinalis* was so named because its petals were used to prepare healing confections that won fame all over Europe for the pharmacists of the French town of Provins, the originators of this flourishing enterprise.

R. x damascena eventually produced the variety *trigintipetala*

Rosa damascena versicolor *("York and Lancaster"), said to have commemorated the end of the Wars of the Roses.*

which, although not the most highly scented, is cultivated on a large scale in the Kazanlŭk valley in Bulgaria as the source of the famed attar of roses. A very old variety of uncertain origin is *R. d. semperflorens*, explicitly so named because it flowers for a second time at the end of the summer—not so remarkable today, but quite unusual in an age when other European roses bloomed only in spring. Some centuries ago *R. x damascena* also produced a mutation or "sport" nowadays called *versicolor* but better known as "York and Lancaster;" the petals have red streaks on a white ground, which has been taken to symbolize the end of the Wars of the Roses and the reconciliation of the Houses of York and Lancaster, whose respective emblems were the white and the red rose.

Probably the most popular of all the many varieties of *R. x damascena* was obtained in 1832 by the curator of the Luxembourg Gardens in Paris, M. Eugène Hardy, who dedicated the rose to his wife. For over half a century (1832–90) the "Mme Hardy" variety, with its highly scented, pure white overlapping petals, like a succession of tiny lapping waves, was the favorite white rose.

R. x alba, third of the trio of ancient garden roses, can still be found in gardens and nurseries in one of its several varieties, all characterized by blue-green foliage and white flowers, sometimes flushed with pink or yellow, and highy scented. They include *R. x a. suaveolens*, *R. x a. maxima* and *R. x a. incarnata*, the last of which perhaps owes a certain degree of its popularity to the various intimate names it has been given, such as "Cuisse de Nymphe" and "Maiden's Blush."

Rapid Progress in the Nineteenth Century

In the early years of the nineteenth century considerable interest was aroused by a repeat-flowering (remontant or recurrent) scarlet-red rose. The bright red color and the recurrent habit suggest that it was derived from *R. chinensis semperflorens*, while the elongated shape of the hips indicates *R.* x *damascena* as the other parent. The unusual color and recurrent character of this rose attracted the attention of the Duchess of Portland during a visit to Italy, and she brought a specimen back to England. This rose was called *R. paestana*, or "Scarlet Four Seasons." In 1807 it reached France, where André Dupont, the gardener to the Empress Josephine, renamed it Duchess of Portland in recognition of her discovery. A dozen or so varieties were obtained, either by natural mutation or from seed, with perfumed flowers and autumn recurrence, creating the so-called Portland roses, which were to enjoy independent status for only a few decades.

The capacity for repeated flowering, introduced into European roses by varieties originating in China, was the outstanding advance which completely altered the traditional use of the flower. In fact, many Chinese varieties had begun to arrive during the last years of the eighteenth century, all of them recurrent and all descended from an ancient species, now latent, named *R. chinensis spontanea*; among these *R. c. semperflorens*, as already mentioned, also possessed the other priceless characteristic of brilliant red petals, unknown until then in Europe. In 1810 the first "tea-scented" varieties arrived in England from Canton, characterized as well by a supple stem bearing petals of a delicate pastel shade.

At that period manual pollination was carried out in a rather disorganized manner; but the availability of both domestic and Asiatic species was an incentive for specialists to grow both types close together and to use seeds that resulted from casual cross-pollination for producing plants with their combined characteristics. Around the middle of the nineteenth century a more rational method of fertilization came into use, the result being the creation of the first *R. chinensis* hybrids.

Around 1817 two such hybrids reached France. One, with clusters of small, light pink flowers, came from the United States. It was called *R.* x *noisettiana* after two brothers named Noisette, one resident in America, the other in France; and it probably originated from the crossing of *R. moschata* (with white flowers at the end of summer) with *R. chinensis pallida* ("Old Blush" or "Parson's Pink China"). The other hybrid came from the island of Réunion, then known as Île Bourbon. The presumed parents

Below: "Jacques Cartier," a Portland rose.
Bottom: "La ReineVictoria," a typical Bourbon rose.

were *R.* x *damascena semperflorens* and an undetermined variety of *R. chinensis*. To commemorate the island from which it originated, the race that derived from it was named Bourbon; it had rounded, perfumed flowers and, like the Noisettes, was moderately recurrent. Successive crosses impaired the distinctive characteristics, and in due course these varieties were absorbed in the category of Hybrid Teas.

The Ancestral Plants

Before the above-mentioned assimilation took place, Bourbon roses, as a result of more or less natural cross-fertilization with Portland roses and hybrids of *R. chinensis*, led to the appearance of repeat-flowering hybrids. These constituted a homogeneous group, increasingly numerous, of shrub roses, plainer than the Chinese varieties, sturdier and more recurrent than the Portlands, and more strongly perfumed than the Bourbons.

Because they flowered twice, in spring and autumn, they came to be known in France as "hybrides remontants" and in England as Hybrid Perpetuals (though the terms "remontant," "repeat-flowering" and "recurrent" are variously used in English to describe their habit). The first variety fully possessing the required attributes was "La Reine," produced in 1842 by the French grower Laffay; within a few years this race of roses had achieved considerable success.

For more than sixty years afterward the Hybrid Perpetuals, thanks to their unquestioned qualities, gained widespread popularity, their sturdy vigor providing the ideal solution wherever harsh winters prevented the cultivation of roses with little resistance to cold, i.e. those broadly described as Tea Roses. The latter, however, were extremely fashionable in the climatically favored zones in and around the French and Italian Mediterranean coasts, where they not only adorned gardens but also provided the opportunity for professional rose-growing activities and, consequently, a large-scale market in cut flowers.

Among the Tea Roses cultivated for this purpose (introduced in 1839 by the French grower Beauregard) was "Safrano," which in the happy climate of Antibes and Bordighera was already blooming in the open at the beginning of April. In addition to its exceptional freedom of flowering, its vigor and the then-unusual color of its petals (saffron, butter-yellow or copper-yellow, depending on the season and soil), "Safrano" was extremely resistant to both drought and disease. Twenty years later, "Maréchal Niel," another famous yellow rose, included among the Noisettes, revealed too much distaste for cold to be counted as a truly ancestral Tea Rose.

Of the simpler recurrent hybrids, there was no more popular variety than "Paul Neyron" (1869), an enormous rose with characteristically bright red petals. In this same group the grower

Antoine Levet of Lyons obtained in 1881 "Ulrich Brunner Fils," a vigorous rose with long branches, beautiful foliage and elegant cherry-red flowers which remained for many years one of the leading varieties for cutting. The year 1887 saw the appearance of "Mrs. John Laing," a lovely English variety with many broad, wavy petals, lilac-pink and perfumed; the celebrated rose grower and breeder Jack Harkness described this as the best of the Hybrid Perpetuals. Two other of the finest roses in this group, as popular with gardeners as with florists, were the cardinal-red "Gloire de Chédane-Guinosseau" and "Frau Karl Druschki" (also called "Reine des Neiges"), the most admired white rose of its time: for half a century it was claimed to have remained unrivaled in Europe in its use for flower arrangements for baptisms, confirmations, first communions and weddings.

In the meantime the most elementary principles of rational rose breeding were beginning to find application, even though the names of the parents of the newly produced varieties were seldom given; the parentage later attributed to them was often the fruit of simple conjecture, at least in the case of the pollinating plant: *mater semper certa, pater dubius.*

Toward the middle of the nineteenth century Hybrid Perpetuals and Tea Roses were considered as potentially ideal pairs, likely to produce promising descendants. Such expectations were based on the possibilities of combining the luminous tints, elegant carriage and strongly recurrent habits of the Teas with the sturdiness, vigor and penetrating scent of the Hybrid Perpetuals.

The progeny of the ensuing multiple marriages constituted the basis of a new race which, after a hesitant start, became firmly established in gardens and, from the beginning of the twentieth century, also among professional growers for the cut-flower trade. After some argument as to which variety deserved recognition as the first of the Hybrid Teas, the decision went to "La France," produced in 1867 by J.B. Guillot of Lyons, although the new race was not officially recognized until 1880.*

This delay in ratification was justified by the great dissimilarity between one flower and another in varieties which ought to have shown complete affinity, and by the low percentage of positive results obtained during those early years. These statistics, attributable to the rare number of planned crosses, are borne out by the very sparse numbers of old Hybrid Teas grown today. Only in the odd nursery or collector's garden is one likely nowadays to come across a few surviving specimens from that initial period, as for example "La France," retained both for its inherent qualities and its importance as ancestral stock; "Captain Christy" (1873), similar in habit to the Perpetual Hybrid varieties; and "Mme Caroline Testout" (1890), because of its exceptional qualities, not least of which is its ability to withstand, unharmed, environmental difficulties and negligence in cultivation.

BASIC SUBDIVISIONS

Yellow Petals for Garden Roses

The Hybrid Teas gradually came to show more refinement in both the quality of flower and plant habit; this was to be seen in the progeny derived from repeated crosses between Teas and hybrids of *R. chinensis*. It was undoubtedly a positive development, but already growers had their sights set on a new goal: a rose suitable both for the garden and the florist which, in addition to the qualities previously achieved by the Hybrid Teas, would have bright yellow petals.

Back at the beginning of the sixteenth century a semi-climbing species with shiny, golden-yellow flowers (*R. foetida* syn. *R. lutea*) had already been introduced from Asia Minor to Europe, but this had a corolla of only five petals, an unattractive characteristic made worse by an unappealing smell. These two factors prevented the species finding a welcome in many gardens. The same faults beset its sport *R. f. bicolor*, which had the upper side of its petals colored nasturtium-red while the underside remained yellow.

---

* The name Hybrides de Thé was officially adopted in France in 1880, but the National Rose Society of Great Britain accepted the name Hybrid Tea only in 1893, after the success obtained everywhere by "Mme Caroline Testout."

Rosa foetida persiana *(from* Flore des serres et des jardins de l'Europe*).*

A century later there was another arrival in Europe from Asia Minor, *R. hemisphaerica*, which had rounded, double sulphur-yellow flowers but bloomed regularly only in hot, dry places; even in these zones it failed to produce seeds, and consequent hybridization could not eliminate these negative features.

During the early years of the nineteenth century two Tea Roses arrived from China (*R. odorata ochroleuca* and *R. odorata pseudindica*); the former had soft yellow petals, the latter yellow petals flushed copper-red and scarlet. Both produced valuable varieties with flowers pleasantly colored but far removed from the desired bright yellow. But there are exceptions to every rule, for already in 1861 the French breeder H. Pradel had put on the market his famous climbing rose "Maréchal Niel," with handsome, scented double flowers, golden-yellow in color; it was descended from the *noisettiana* variety (already mentioned), but among its more recent ancestors was *R. o. pseudindica*, the Tea with copper-yellow double flowers. The flower was inclined to droop its head on a weak stem, the plant lost its vigor in very cold climates, and the blooms rotted in periods of persistent rain; however, "Maréchal Niel" represented an important advance, even though it was a climber and not a shrub.

The privilege of imbuing shrub roses with the bright yellow of its petals went to a large double-flowered form of *R. foetida, R. f. persiana*, introduced into Europe in around 1840; the color range and the balanced, vigorous growth of the bush attracted the attention of more enterprising growers. The most determined of these was a young but already experienced breeder, Joseph Pernet-Ducher of Lyons, who refused to be discouraged by fruitless attempts at obtaining fertile seeds. Eventually, the crossing of a Perpetual Hybrid variety ("Antoine Ducher") with *R. f. persiana* produced, in 1900, a bush rose with perfumed double flowers which displayed the hoped-for bright yellow color mingled with touches of orange and pink; it was named "Soleil d'Or." Because it had few branches and was not markedly recurrent, it was used almost exclusively to transmit its color through crosses. Ten years later, Joseph Pernet-Ducher himself obtained "Rayon d'Or," with uniformly golden-yellow flowers, by fertilizing another of its varieties with pollen from "Soleil d'Or;" unlike its parent, "Rayon d'Or" had a strong constitution and well-balanced growth habit.

In the last catalogs to list the Pernetianas as a separate family of roses, we find "Talisman" (1929), golden-yellow flushed with red, and the multicolored "President Herbert Hoover" (1930), with orange-yellow, pink and copper-red petals, strong and divergent growth, and flowers on long stems; one of its sports ("Texas Centennial") has the same habit but differs in its red petals enlivened at the base with yellow.

Joseph Pernet-Ducher continued in his chosen path and produced further successes with new varieties of Pernetianas; the loveliest varieties of that early period were "Souvenir de Claudius Pernet" and "Souvenir de Julien Pernet"—both dedicated to his sons, who died in World War I—"Julien Potin," etc.

The Large-Flowered Roses

At the beginning of the present century the Hybrid Teas had not only acquired new colors but had also improved in appearance. This was not surprising since, if we glance at the rose family tree, we find that the antecedents included, in addition to the Pernetianas and *R. odorata* (i.e. the Tea Rose), diverse hybrids of *R. chinensis*, Portlands, Noisettes and Bourbons, all of which at various times combined to create the Hybrid Perpetuals and the Hybrid Teas.

Some rose specialists now began to ask themselves whether the term "Hybrid Tea" was still quite suitable or whether the presence of other stocks was not gradually invalidating the name. Many years were to pass, however, before the problem was seriously examined, let alone fully resolved, even by the World Federation of Rose Societies. The proposal that received the most votes was the English, which suggested that the Hybrid Teas should henceforth be given the new name of Large-Flowered Roses.

The variety which perhaps more than any other signaled the novel characteristics of the Hybrid Teas was "Ophelia" (W. Paul, 1912). The flower retained its slender shape even when fully

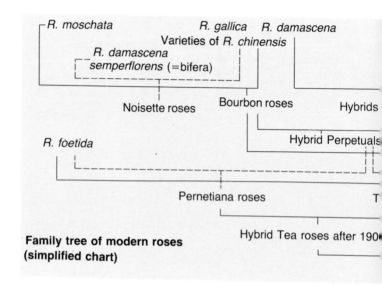

Family tree of modern roses (simplified chart)

R. moschata

R. gallica   R. damascena

Varieties of R. chinensis

R. damascena
semperflorens (=bifera)

Noisette roses   Bourbon roses   Hybrids

R. foetida   Hybrid Perpetuals

Pernetiana roses   T

Hybrid Tea roses after 190⬛

opened, and the beautiful pinkish-white petals were delicately scented. The bush form of "Ophelia" has virtually vanished from modern gardens, but the vigorous climbing form is still much admired.

"Ophelia" has gained a special place in rose history for having produced, through successive crosses, many excellent varieties ("Talisman," "Columbia," "Mrs. Pierre S. du Pont," etc.) and—exceptionally—for having created more than twenty sports (among them "Mme Butterfly" proved particularly popular); they, in their turn, tended to produce more sports. Consequently, a large number of roses dating from that period are descended from "Ophelia."

After the Pernetianas lost their independent nomenclature, it was the Hybrid Teas which inherited their most notable qualities, i.e. the yellow, copper and flame tones, individually or mixed. Among these were "Talisman," with red and yellow parents (The Montgomery Co., U.S.A., 1929), the vigorous "President Herbert Hoover," orange, pink and yellow (Coddington, U.S.A., 1930), and the Dutch variety "Comtesse Vandal" (M. Leenders, 1932), with handsomely colored corollas, chamois-yellow above, copper-red below. Several years later the Pernetiana features were stunningly displayed in "Condesa de Sàstago" (Pedro Dot, Spain, 1932), a typical example of a variety with clearly defined bicolor flowers: its glowing petals appeared to represent, on either surface, the yellow and the red of the Spanish flag. Many rose breeders then proceeded to concentrate on the Pernetiana

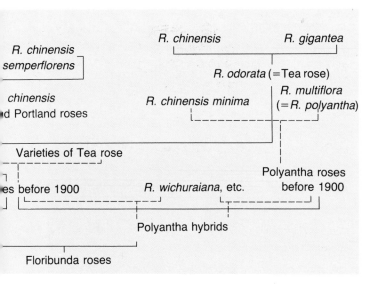

R. chinensis

R. gigantea

R. chinensis semperflorens

R. odorata (=Tea rose)

chinensis

R. chinensis minima

R. multiflora (=R. polyantha)

d Portland roses

Varieties of Tea rose

es before 1900

R. wichuraiana, etc.

Polyantha roses before 1900

Polyantha hybrids

Floribunda roses

colors, and in 1936 the French-American J.H. Nicolas had a resounding success with "Eclipse," its elongated, pure yellow corollas sweetly scented; while Charles Mallerin, the retired railway engineer who, although an amateur, ended his career as a skilled rose breeder with the Meillands, won the gold medal at the prestigious international trials of 1936 at Bagatelle with "Mme Henri Guillot," its petals a glowing blend of orange, coral and nasturtium-red.

By this time rose breeding had become both something of an art and a science; pollination was no longer attempted without a prior study of the likely attributes to be passed on from one generation to another. Although it was still impossible to predict exactly what the result of a particular cross might be, given the large number of unknown antecedents, so that a strong element of chance was still involved, the possibilities of success were much enhanced by eliminating uncontrolled breeding experiments.

Using the same ancestors ("Julien Potin," a Pernetiana, and "Sensation," a Hybrid Tea), two Mediterranean rose breeders, the Italian Domenico Aicardi in 1936 and the Spaniard Pedro Dot in 1939 respectively, obtained "Signora Piero Puricelli" (syn. "Signora") and "Marquesa de Urquijo" (syn. "Pilar Landecho"), two varieties which were alone enough to make both men famous.

We have already mentioned the influence exerted on the Hybrid Teas by the chromosomes of R. foetida persiana as

"Peace," the first rose described as the "World's Favorite Rose."

confirmation of the theory that the intervention of a new species may have a beneficial effect. Further proof of this comes from the renowned "Peace." In fact, *R. f. persiana* and its descendant "Souvenir de Claudius Pernet" (as well as some Hybrid Perpetuals and their antecedents) figured among the ancestors of this variety which, by virtue of its opulence and color—the flowers superb as soon as they open and remaining magnificent even as they slowly fade—its large, glossy leaves and its vigorous, branching growth, has been called the "rose of the century."

Francis, the twenty-two-year-old son of the Lyons rose grower Antoine Meilland, could have had no idea that one of the numerous pollinations carried out would result in 1935 in the first flowering of this astonishing variety. After four years of trials, he was convinced that his earlier expectations had been far surpassed. The outbreak of war hampered its immediate international distribution, and it was eventually marketed under various names: "Mme Antoine Meilland" in France and French-speaking countries, "Gioia" in Italy, "Gloria Dei" in Germany, and "Peace" in America—this last name, by happy coincidence, being officially ratified on April 29, 1945, the day Berlin fell to the Allies. Three years previously, in the park of La Tête d'Or in Lyons, the new variety had been hailed as "the most beautiful rose in France."

After the war ended some time passed before international rose growers, having replenished their stocks and distributed their new catalogs, resumed normal activities so that gardens could recover their former splendor. "Peace," under its various names, now brushed aside all opposition; by 1950 some thirty million plants were growing in every part of the world!

The World Federation of Rose Societies, during the conference held at Oxford in 1976, called "Peace" the "World's Favorite Rose," this being the first variety to receive such recognition, thereafter awarded every two years to the rose obtaining the most votes from the fifteen associations belonging to the Federation. "Peace" bequeathed many of its qualities to its descendants, notably its vigor, its consistently glossy foliage and its distinctive flower color.

In 1941 the sole winner of the second edition of the All-America Rose Selection, the American trials for new roses, was "Charlotte Armstrong." This variety, with its long, deep pink petals, was introduced from California in 1940. During and after the war it had a decisive influence on American rose production; and its qualities were transmitted to "Queen Elizabeth," which in 1979 was awarded the title of "World's Favorite Rose"; "Sutter's Gold," "First Love," "Mojave," "Pink Parfait" and dozens of other excellent varieties.

The parents of "Charlotte Armstrong" were "Sœur Thérèse" and "Crimson Glory," which in their turn were descended from "Souvenir de Claudius Pernet" and "Mme Caroline Testout"—an indication of the influence exerted by the Pernetianas on the evolution of the modern rose.

Some years after the acclaimed arrival of "Peace" and "Charlotte Armstrong" another rose was introduced by the German grower Wilhelm Kordes; in Germany it was called "Sondermeldung," elsewhere "Independence." It was notable for its resistance to disease and its remarkable color, never previously seen and variously described as red lead, sealing-wax red, etc. Yet despite the unqualified welcome it received for these two attributes, it was criticized in some quarters because of the crude color assumed by the petals before fading, its uncertain classification (not a Floribunda, having too few flowers, and not a Hybrid Tea, since the flowers were not big enough), and its weak stem. It was thus an unexceptional rose for the garden but superlative for breeding, initiating a prolific series of varieties with orange petals. Among the descendants of "Independence" were "Soraya," "Tropicana," "Baccara" and "Alexander."

From Orange and Red to Blue and Black

Those were the years when breeders started looking for a blue rose—a still far-distant goal—since although a lot of interesting work has been carried out, the fact remains that this color is not part of the rose's chromosomal makeup and is unlikely to be so in the future. Jack Harkness commented that "all the so-called blue roses are in truth failed reds or pinks."

The first so-called blue roses to be listed after the war were given somewhat timid and unrevealing names such as "Prelude" (1945) and "Tristesse" (1951); but in due course there was a helpful indication of color, as in "Lilac Time" (1945), "Sterling Silver" (1962), "Heure Mauve" (1962) and "Lilac Charm" (1962). In 1964 the breeder Mathias Tantau introduced a variety with beautifully fashioned and highly perfumed flowers, their color described variously as steel-blue and silver-lilac. It was called "Mainzer Fastnacht" in Germany, "Sissi" in France and "Blue Moon" in other countries. For over twenty years it held its own against subsequent rivals ("Nil Bleu," "Lady X," "Violetera," "Charles de Gaulle," etc.) and even today competes with the newest arrivals, including the highly scented "Dioressence" (Delbard), "Jacaranda" (Kordes) and the violet-red "Blue River," also from Kordes.

There is a strange discontinuity of varieties with violet petals. First reports go back to the middle of the nineteenth century, and after a silence of some fifty years they reemerged between 1905 and 1924, as is shown by the following short list which points to their virtually complete disappearance in recent years: "Cardinal de Richelieu," Gallica, M. Laffay, 1840; "Reine des Violettes," Hybrid Perpetual, Mille-Mallet, 1860; "Hansa," Rugosa, Schaum-Van Tol, 1905; "Blue Magenta," Climbing Multiflora, 1907; "Veilchenblau," Climbing Multiflora, J.C. Schmidt, 1909; Violetta," Climbing Multiflora, E. Turbat, 1921; "Baby Faraux," Dwarf Polyantha, L. Lille, 1924; "Rose Marie Viaud," Climbing Multiflora, Igoult, 1924.

Despite so many difficulties, it is just possible that one day we shall see, in defiance of genetic laws, a rose with blue petals; a true black rose is far less likely, and it must be admitted that few tears would be shed if this continued to be so. After all, it is often said that only flowers with light, luminous colors assist nature by attracting the pollinating insects necessary for continuing the species.

As with tulips and gladioli, the so-called black varieties are not really black, but very dark shades of red or brown. The first modern rose with reddish-black petals was probably "Château de Clos Vougeot," a Hybrid Tea produced at the beginning of the present century by Joseph Pernet-Ducher. It is a none too sturdy bush of divergent habit, and the considerable renown it once enjoyed was due to its unusual color and its penetrating perfume; nowadays it is of purely historical interest.

Here, for collectors, is a chronological list of a couple of dozen Hybrid Teas bearing red petals flushed with black: "Château de Clos Vougeot," J. Pernet-Ducher, 1908; "Admiral Ward," J. Pernet-Ducher, 1915; "Gloire de Hollande," Verschuren & Zonen, 1919; "Ami Quinard," Ch. Mallerin, 1930; "Catherine Kordes," W. Kordes, 1930; "Night," S. McGredy, 1930; "Black Knight," V.S. Hilloch, 1934; "Crimson Glory," W. Kordes, 1935;

Typical shape of a Hybrid Tea rose.

"Lemania," E. Heizmann, 1936; "Jane Thorton," Bees Ltd., 1940; "Tassin," F. Meilland, 1942; "Congo," Ch. Mallerin, 1943; "Charles Mallerin," F. Meilland, 1947; "Josephine Bruce," Bees Ltd., 1949; "Super Congo," F. Meilland, 1950; "Chrysler Imperial," W.E. Lammerts, 1952; "Papa Meilland," A. Meilland, 1963; "Bonne Nuit," M. Combe, 1966; "Norita," M. Combe, 1971; "Black Night," R. Huber, 1973; "Black Lady," Tantau, 1976; "Perle Noire," G. Delbard, 1980; "Le Rouge et le Noir," G. Delbard, 1982; and, in the same class of Hybrid Teas, the following climbing varieties: "Lemania," E. Heizmann, 1937; "Guinée," Ch. Mallerin, 1938; and "Don Juan," M. Malandrone, 1958.

Swift Development

The first half of the nineteenth century is generally regarded as the departure point for the rapid modern evolution of the genus *Rosa*; it is not surprising, therefore, that in 1985 the Royal National Rose Society decided to bring out a graded list of roses more than a century old and still being cultivated. The first four, in order of popularity, were *R. gallica versicolor*, better known by its common name of "Rosa Mundi," the climber "Zéphirine Drouhin," descended from *R.* x *borboniana*, "Mme Hardy," hybrid of *R.* x *damascena*, and "Cécile Brunner" (with *R. chinensis* as one of its antecedents), recurrent, fragrant, with splendidly formed miniature flowers.

A corner of the rose garden of Haÿ-les-Roses.

The publication is further proof of the endurance of old roses and the increasing interest in them shown by serious growers attracted to the shape of the corollas, the scent of the petals, the blue-green color of some of the leaves, and the awareness that there is always the risk of this or that variety disappearing.

It is most important that old roses be grown separately from modern varieties. Thanks to continuous selective breeding, the latter have acquired qualities that were once lacking or barely evident; at the same time, however, subsequent transformations have done away with some of the features that give the older varieties their charm.

Jules Gravereaux, founder of the historic garden of Haÿ-les-Roses, was the most experienced grower at the turn of the last century, and once remarked that a rose garden that did not have a place for the old varieties was like a beautiful but silly woman.

Having discussed in broad terms the Hybrid Teas of former years as well as roses with unusual colors, let us now consider some of the varieties which have been introduced since World War II. For convenience, they are listed here in three groups representing successive decades (from 1945 to 1974), for comparison with the roses of the present day.

Despite the best of intentions, the following lists necessarily omit a large number of interesting varieties; those included have been selected merely as representative examples. Some of the varieties, together with a good number of others deserving mention, are discussed at greater length, including details of their essential characteristics, in the accompanying individual illustrated entries.

HT varieties (single-flowered or large-flowered) representative of the decade 1945–54
"Michèle Meilland," light pink, Meilland, France 1945
"Ena Harkness," bright red, Norman, U.K. 1946
"Opéra," red with yellow base, Gaujard, France 1949
"Madame Kriloff," orange-yellow with pink veining, Meilland, France 1949
"Grand-mère Jenny," yellow flushed carmine, Meilland, France 1950
"Karl Herbst," red, Kordes, Federal Republic of Germany 1950
"Sutter's Gold," yellow flushed orange-pink, Swim, U.S.A. 1950
"First Love," deep pink, Swim, U.S.A. 1951
"Chrysler Imperial," dark red, Lammerts, U.S.A. 1952
"Tiffany," tones of pink, Lindquist, U.S.A. 1954.

HT varieties (single-flowered or large-flowered) representative of the decade 1955–64
"Kordes Perfecta," creamy white and red, Kordes, Federal Republic of Germany 1957
"Rose Gaujard," red with pink and silver reverse, Gaujard, France 1957

"Wendy Cussons," deep pink, Gregory, U.K. 1959
"Piccadilly," red with yellow reverse, McGredy, Northern Ireland 1960
"Tropicana," coral orange, Tantau, Federal Republic of Germany 1960
"Papa Meilland," dark red, Meilland, France 1963
"Pascali," white, Lens, Belgium 1963
"Fragrant Cloud," (syn. "Duftwolke," "Nuage Parfumé"), coral red, Tantau, Federal Republic of Germany 1964
"Blue Moon," (syn. "Mainzer Fastnacht," "Sissi"), silver-lilac, Tantau, Federal Republic of Germany 1964
"Mister Lincoln," dark red, Swim & Weeks, U.S.A. 1964.

HT varieties (single-flowered or large-flowered) representative of the decade 1965–74
"Ernst H. Morse," dark red, Kordes, Federal Republic of Germany 1965
"Grandpa Dickson," Light yellow flushed pink, Dickson, Northern Ireland 1966
"Lady X," lilac-mauve, Meilland, France 1966
"Versailles" (syn. "Castel"), mother-of-pearl pink, Delbard, France 1967
"First Prize," ivory with pink flushed edges, Boerner, U.S.A. 1970
"Sunblest" (syn. "Landora"), yellow, Tantau, Federal Republic of Germany 1970
"Alexander" (syn. "Alexandra"), vermilion, Harkness, U.K. 1972
"Grand Nord," white, Delbard, France 1973*
"Lily de Gerlache," dark pink, Inst. Plantes Orn. Li., Belgium 1973
"Sonia Meilland," light pink, Meilland, France 1973

All the above-mentioned varieties have earned a prominent place in the history of modern roses after long years of trials and tests, whereas the varieties of more recent times are necessarily evaluated with greater caution, initial judgments sometimes being revised. In fact, the combined effects of climate, soil and latitude may exert a significant influence on the yield of individual varieties and often, with the passage of time, have unexpected consequences. So when trying to assess the suitability of a rose, buyers have to make sure that the climatic and soil conditions from which it comes are as similar as may be to those of the site for which it is destined.

In order to give potential buyers useful information about the effects of environment, many new roses obtained from breeders of various nations are grown for a couple of years in experimental beds under different climatic conditions. We shall return to this subject later, so need mention here only that some dozen

---

* For about twenty years the technical director in charge of breeding Delbard roses has been André Chabert.

countries in Europe are involved, from Spain to Italy in the south, and from Ireland to Holland in the north. Such comparisons will therefore help buyers to come to conclusions, always bearing in mind that some breeders may choose not to submit their novelties or may send them to certain centers and not to others.

Given such reservations, here are descriptive comments on some of the HT varieties marketed during the decade 1975–85, starting with those from the United States.

"Double Delight," with creamy white petals edged cherry-red, was in 1977 deemed worthy of the All-America Rose Selection, the top American award, and in 1985, at the World Rose Conference in Toronto, was included in the list of the World's Favorite Rose. Previously it had also won awards in Europe— gold medals at Rome and Baden Baden and a prize for perfume at Geneva and The Hague. In spite of these awards, however, the results in some zones were not those that might have been expected.

"Paradise," also given the award (in 1978) of the All-America Rose Selection, is notable for its original bright lilac-pink margins.

"Pristine," with gleaming ivory-white petals, won the gold medal in the 1980 Premio Roma and the silver at Monza in the same year.

For some years new introductions from Sam McGredy have been arriving, not from Northern Ireland as of old, but from New Zealand. "Olympiad," described as maintaining its solid red color from start to finish, was one of the trio of winners of the All-America Rose Selection of 1984 and was included among the official symbols of that year's Olympic Games. Sam McGredy is now venturing into new territory with his "hand-painted roses."

The two major German firms of rose growers are concentrating on varieties which in addition to the traditional requirements also have a strong scent—"Duftgold" (Tantau 1981, golden-yellow) and "Duftzauber" (Kordes 1984, glowing red)—and, where unusual colors are concerned, "Esmeralda," syn. "Keepsake" (Kordes 1981, pink), "Jacaranda" (Kordes 1985, lilac) and "Black Lady" (Tantau 1976, reddish-black).

"Silver Jubilee" (Cocker, Aberdeen 1978), pink and cream, headed the Royal National Rose Society's classification for

(*) Points	Variety	Year	Type
365	Pink Favorite	1956	HT
272	Silver Jubilee	1978	HT
160	Peace	1942	HT
119	Red Devil	1967	HT
103	Southampton	1972	FL
97	Rose Gaujard	1958	HT
86	Grandpa Dickson	1966	HT
59	Alexander	1972	HT
59	Honey Favorite	1962	HT
44	Wendy Cussons	1959	HT

Hybrid Teas; later came "Sweetheart," a posthumous variety also from Alec Cocker (1982).

Jack Harkness, in his excellent book *Roses*, awards a maximum of five stars (applying the system usually reserved for hotels) to the finest roses of every type, period and provenance (up to 1978); and of these most recent varieties he includes two from the above list, "Sonia Meilland" and "Wendy Cussons." He gives four stars to "Alexander," the vermilion rose that he himself introduced in 1972.

France has kept alive its excellent reputation for famous roses. From Meilland have come "Princesse de Monaco" (1982, creamy white with red flushed margins), "Louis de Funès" (1983, red and yellow bicolored), "Yves Piaget" ("Neyron" pink, 1984), a rose that resembles a highly scented peony, etc. Georges Delbard, the other "great name," has also kept up the standards: his most recent success has been "Mme Georges Delbard" (1985), described as the reddest of reds, but others have included "Dioressence" (1984), "the highly scented blue rose," "Satellite" (coral-red, 1982), "Epidor" (yellow, 1980), "Grand Siècle" (milk-white and soft pink, 1977), "La Marseillaise" (blackcurrant-red, 1976) and "Nil Bleu" (lilac-mauve, 1975).

Before concluding this essentially brief survey, we should at least record the names of Laperrière, Jean Gaujard—who has continued the former business of Pernet-Ducher—and Combe, Croix, Dorieux, Eve Kriloff, Orard, Pekmez and Pineau, representative of successive generations of French rose breeders.

Among other very active European breeders are Cants, Fryers, Le Grice and Mattock in the United Kingdom, Poulsen in Denmark, Lens in Belgium, De Ruiter and Interplant in Holland, Dot in Spain, Cazzaniga, Mansuino and others in Italy. All are conscious of the fact that the modern generation of rose breeders cannot restrict itself to crosses of successful varieties but must concentrate as well on new species and varieties in the hope of transmitting to the progeny qualities capable of still further improvement: propagation by cuttings, elimination or reduction of thorns, cultivation in containers, increasing recurrence in climbing roses, resistance to a wide range of diseases, etc.

With regard to the last, it is significant that in a list published in 1985 by the Royal National Rose Society, comprising the ten varieties most resistant to disease, only three were introduced commercially in the 1970s, all the others previously.* Although these findings apply only to the United Kingdom, it is possible to deduce that compared with the undeniable successes achieved in the duration of flowering, color and perfume, etc., relatively little progress has been made in the defense against plant parasites. The conclusion must be that the rose breeder cannot afford to improvise but has to rely on preparatory genetic work and careful planning.

For some years it has been apparent that the name Hybrid Tea

"Perle d'Or," a rose with small flowers and vigorous growth.

is no longer botanically acceptable; the new classification word introduced for Hybrid Tea is Large-Flowered rose, although—as with Cluster-Flowered rose for Floribunda—this new term is by no means universally accepted.

Uses for Hybrid Teas

The roses we have so far examined have a dual habit, that of forming bushes with elegant flowers (traditionally described as Hybrid Teas) and of being capable, at least in the first flowering period, of producing stems with single flowers that can be cut. It is sensible, however, to think in terms of either rather then both. Since such roses are prized more for the quality than the quantity of their flowers, it has to be admitted that they give their most decorative show when all flowers are left on the plant. Flowers for cutting should be reserved for those varieties best suited for the purpose, grown in an area not intended for display. In either instance it is as well for groups to be made up of one variety; the patch of color will be far more effective than if constituted of different hues, and in the case of cut flowers particularly, it is essential to concentrate on corollas of the same color and form.

Some growers choose their varieties for the quality of their scent. Today, as in the past, some roses are highly perfumed and others odorless, and it is important that catalogs emphasize this point.

Rose lovers who prefer not to cut flowers from bushes planted

to adorn the garden find support in the fact that the roses which keep best and are therefore most suitable for cutting are seldom scented, since to a large extent their long duration depends on the firm consistency of the petals, a condition which inhibits fragrance. Roses sold by florists therefore last a long time but have little or no scent. When cutting flowers it is best to make the cut more or less in the middle part of the stem immediately above a shoot facing outward from the bush.

The length of the bed in which plants are to be grown depends solely on the amount of available space and on personal choice; but to facilitate watering, weeding, hoeing and feeding it is advisable not to plant more than three bushes in every row. The breadth of each row will vary between 1.5 m. (5 ft.) and just under 2 m. (6 ft.), depending on the habit and strength of the bushes.

Multiflora, Polyantha and Floribunda

In 1784 the Swedish botanist Carl Peter Thunberg discovered in Japan a hardy climbing species of the genus *Rosa* which he named *R. multiflora*; its inflorescences were made up of many single white flowers in pyramidal, nonrecurrent clusters. Exactly sixty years later the German botanists Siebold and Zuccarini, unaware of the previous discovery, gave the same species, which they too had found, the name *R. polyantha*, the Greek form of the preceding nomenclature.

It is the rule in botanical nomenclature for priority to be given to the first name validly published; but as we shall soon see, even in the botanical field it is sometimes difficult for the laws to be applied.

In the second half of the nineteenth century Lyons was the home of a number of active and experienced French growers and breeders, then the most renowned in Europe; they included Bernaix, Dubreuil, Ducher, Guillot, Pernet-Ducher and Rambaud. Each vied with the other to produce the first remontant shrub rose with small double flowers; but it is reliably reported that in around 1865 the grower Jean Baptiste Guillot (Guillot Fils) acquired seeds of *R. multiflora*, and that repeated sowings produced bushes that were of low stature and recurrent (characteristics reputedly attained from a cross, probably in the country of origin, between the climbing *R. multiflora* and *R. chinensis minima*). These characteristics were subsequently manifested in seedlings of the second generation.

Among these, one stood out for its small size and double white flowers (each a couple of centimeters across) in clusters; Guillot was so impressed by it that he put it on the market with the name "Pâquerette." In 1881 the same breeder introduced a second rose which was notable only for its pink color, calling it "Mignonette."

"Pâquerette" was therefore the founder of the race of roses which became known all over the world—contrary to the nomenclature rule—not as *multiflora* but as *polyantha*.

Other varieties followed, all obtained by crosses between "polyanthas": "Gloire des Polyantha," 1887, bright pink; "Marie Pavié," 1888, light pink, perfumed; "Katharine Zeimet," 1901, pure white, perfumed, and many others.

The following are some of the characteristics of this new race: small flowers (2–4 cm. in diameter), usually flattened, single or double in tight clusters, blooming from spring to autumn; leaves rough and opaque. Absence of such identifying signs, the slender shape of the flowers and small, pointed leaves led to two or three of the most admired small-flower varieties ("Cécile Brunner," 1880 and "Perle d'Or," 1883) being transferred to another group (hybrids of *R. chinensis*); earlier these had been included because one of the parents was presumed to be a descendant of *R. multiflora*, but it was in fact the other parent which transmitted the morphological and genetic influence.

The important step of giving the petals the bright red color they had so far lacked was taken by Théodore Levavasseur, a skilled Breton rose breeder who later moved to Orléans. In 1893 there arrived from Japan the first climbing rose with glowing red flowers arranged in huge pyramidal clusters; it was called "Crimson Conquest" and was probably a hybrid of *R. multiflora* and *R. wichuraiana*. Levavasseur confidently proceeded to pollinate "Crimson Conquest" with "Gloire des Polyantha," succeeding in producing a sturdy shrub which, among other attributes, had low growth and masses of crimson flowers, markedly recurrent; this he named "Mme Norbert Levavasseur," in tribute to the young wife of one of his business partners. This variety (1903) was to become the parent of a large family both through crosses ("Orléans Rose," 1909; "Ellen Poulsen," 1911) and through sports,* a faculty strongly displayed even in "Orléans Rose," creating among others, "Miss Edith Cavell," 1917 and "Coral Cluster," 1921.

Although attempts had already been made before 1924 to cross Polyantha roses with varieties of *R. chinensis* (e.g. "Cécile Brunner"), of *R. wichuraiana* (e.g. "Yvonne Rabier") and of Hybrid Teas (e.g. "Joseph Guy"="La Fayette"), it was in that year that the Danish grower Svend Poulsen, continuing the work of his father, obtained his first rose which was—like the previous Polyanthas—resistant to cold but sturdier, with an upright habit, smooth foliage and large flower clusters in glowing colors. This was achieved with "Else Poulsen" (bright pink) and the next year with "Kirsten Poulsen" (single carmine-pink), both fruit of the marriage between "Orléans Rose" and "Red Star," a Hybrid Tea with red flowers; by virtue of habit, and size and color of flowers, the two Poulsen varieties are regarded as the first Hybrid Polyanthas, which played an important role in the years that followed by producing fine varieties such as those early successes "Donald Prior" (1930), "Betty Prior" (1934) and "Baby Château" (1936), a modest garden shrub, but parent of a progeny which eventually attained the desired scarlet color.

This was the magic moment for the Hybrid Polyanthas, with a succession of varieties, some of them quite unforgettable: "Dagmar Späth" (sport of "Joseph Guy"), "Dainty Maid" (with scented flowers) and "Orange Triumph" (mother of many descendants).

Finally, in 1938, forty years after the appearance of the first yellow Hybrid Tea, the first Hybrid Polyantha with more or less yellow petals, "Poulsen Yellow," was introduced, followed in 1939 by "Minna Kordes," which owed much of its popularity to its American name of "World's Fair," to commemorate the great exhibition held that year in New York.

There was also "Independence" (syn. "Kordes Sondermeldung"), with petals that were vermilion, a color once furnished by the cochineal (*vermiculus*) but never previously applied to the

---

* The term "sport," suggesting some whim on the part of the plant, is used to describe a mutation due to an alteration to the genes and chromosomes which control a particular characteristic: in roses it almost always affects the color of the petals or the habit of the plant (e.g. from shrub to climber). In Polyantha roses, more frequently than elsewhere, the variety obtained through such a mutation tends to reassume the original characteristic (e.g. petal color). In some instances the tendency to produce sports is also exhibited in successive generations (a typical example is "Orléans Rose"); research by Professor S.G. Saakov of the Leningrad Botanical Institute has shown that this variety produced 24 direct sports and that these, in their turn, produced 14 more. A variety produced by such a mutation can be propagated by grafts, cuttings and layering.

Below: "Märchenland," a vigorous rose with a habit midway between that of a bush and a shrub.
Bottom: "Rosemary Rose," a modern version of an old-fashioned rose.

petals of a rose. Official records say that it was put on the market in 1949, but back in 1943 it had won the gold medal at the Bagatelle trials; daughter of "Crimson Glory" and "Baby Château," like the latter it was a nondescript garden rose, but it had the privilege of passing down to descendants the pigment pelargonidum, responsible for the color, now possessed by many roses, variously described in catalogs as geranium-red, cinnabar, red lead, scarlet, orange-scarlet, etc.

At more or less this time the commercial name "Floribunda" (which for some years had already replaced that of Hybrid Polyantha in America) began to be adopted as well in Europe; at first it was seldom applied but it soon became accepted, especially when—through repeated crosses with Hybrid Teas—the flowers, although still in clusters, tended to take on the shape of the latter.

Throughout the world there was wide acclaim and enthusiasm for Floribundas such as "Goldilocks" (1945), with its decorative pure yellow flowers; "Frensham" (1946), raised by Albert Norman in England and for many years adjudged Britain's best Floribunda; and "Alain" (1946), the French counterpart of "Frensham." "Lavender Pinocchio" (1948) excited much interest with its new color, its lilac-pink petals delicately fragrant. "Fashion" (1949) aroused surprise and admiration, too, for its novel salmon-peach color and well-shaped flowers. "Masquerade" (1949) created a sensation when it appeared, with its changing colors of yellow, pink and red; it was possibly descended from R. chinensis mutabilis, but its complex genetic origins were enhanced by an intermediate series of excellent antecedents. "Red Favorite"="Schweizer Gruss"="Höllanderin" (1951) was a low, much-branched bush with shining dark red flower clusters, while "Märchenland," with glossy foliage and masses of pink flowers, was almost shrub-like in habit.

Still another type of free-flowering rose is the majestic Grandiflora. This is not recognized as a distinct type in the U.K. (where it is considered just a sub-class of the Floribundas) but has for long been ranked as a distinct class of rose in the United States.

The Grandiflora is a cross between Hybrid Teas and Floribundas. It is taller and hardier than the Hybrid Teas, and has larger flowers borne on longer stems than the Floribundas. On the other hand, the flowers are slightly smaller than those of the Hybrid Teas. The flowers are borne in clusters and also singly.

Examples of the Grandiflora include the magnificent "Queen Elizabeth," "Montezuma" and "White Lightnin'." Several well known roses that were once classified in the U.S. as Hybrid Teas have been reclassified as Grandifloras. These include Duet, Gay Princess and Granada.

The year 1954 is remembered for the introduction to gardens of "Rosemary Rose," described as a "modern edition of an ancient rose," and "Spartan," free-flowering and recurrent as befits a Floribunda, but with blooms like those of a Hybrid Tea. The milestone, however, was to be "Queen Elizabeth," bred from

Below: "Europeana," a Floribunda valued for its cut flowers.
Page 42: "Mme Dimitriu," a much-admired Polyantha variety.

"Charlotte Armstrong" and "Floradora," and astonishing for its vigor, habit, gleaming petals, elegant flowers on strong stems, abundance of blooms and recurrence. The first variety officially described as World's Favorite Rose was "Peace," but the next rose to receive this award was "Queen Elizabeth."

This variety marked an important stage in rose evolution: the large, well-formed flowers, almost always in clusters, and the male parent ("Floradora") suggested inclusion among the Floribundas, but its ability to flourish both as a single specimen and as a constituent of a dense, tall hedge persuaded the Americans, when it was commercially launched in the United States, to give "Queen Elizabeth" a new category known as Grandiflora. This name did not prove generally acceptable to European growers; they had previously reluctantly agreed to the term Floribunda and now, rather than use the new denomination, preferred to qualify Floribunda in such cases with the description "Hybrid Tea type."

More than thirty years have elapsed since then, but agreement has still not been reached.

Varieties subsequently included among the Grandifloras were mostly of American origin ("Montezuma," "Carrousel," "Olé," "Pink Parfait," etc.) but there were also "Miss France" and "Sonia Meilland" from France, and various hybrids from other breeders— Kordes and Tantau from the Federal Republic of Germany— which were often classified as Grandiflora in the United States and as Hybrid Tea or Floribunda in the countries of origin.

Two years after the commercial introduction of the exceptionally vigorous "Queen Elizabeth," it was the turn of "Allgold," small and with all the major requirements: warm golden-yellow flowers that do not fade, produced in abundance and quickly recurrent, shining leaves and branching growth—attributes to rival those of any modern variety.

In 1957 "Sarabande" appeared, another low-growing bush but one with an open habit, notable for its semi-double flowers with a dozen or so large orange-scarlet petals; softer in tone was the scented "Orange Sensation" (De Ruiter, Holland, 1960).

Meanwhile "Iceberg" ("Schneewittchen" in Germany, "Fée des Neiges" in France) was winning great acclaim everywhere. At the sixth international gathering of rose societies in 1983 it was designated World's Favorite Rose.

"Lilli Marlene" (1959) was an excellent small-sized rose similar to "Zambra" (1961), rich with pale orange and yellow flowers. "Europeana" (1963) had so many flower clusters as to give the plant a much more spreading appearance than was actually the case.

The Cluster-Flowered roses (as Floribundas are now named) are playing an increasingly important role both in private and public gardens. In the past it was impossible to obtain the broad patches of color, of long duration, that only they can provide; and the gap is gradually narrowing between these and the Hybrid Teas which once reigned supreme.

The most important novelties of the last twenty years or there-

abouts include "Pariser Charm," Tantau, Federal Republic of Germany; "Mme Dimitriu," Delbard, France; "Sangria," Meilland, France; "Elizabeth of Glamis"="Irish Beauty," McGredy, New Zealand; and "Scented Air," Dickson, U.K.—all varieties still to be reckoned with. Then came "Picasso" (1971); "Old Master" and "Matangi" (1974), the first hand-painted roses from McGredy, New Zealand; "Shocking Blue" and "Friesia"="Sunsprite," Kordes, Federal Republic of Germany, 1974; "Montana," Tantau, Federal Republic of Germany, 1974; "Candeur," Delbard, France, 1974; "Margaret Merril," Harkness, U.K., 1977; "Priscilla Burton," McGredy, New Zealand, 1978; "La Sevillana," Meilland, France, 1978; "Manou," Meilland, France, 1979; "Maria-Mathilda," Lens, Belgium, 1980; "Anne Harkness," Harkness, U.K., 1983; "Céline Delbard," Delbard, France, 1983; "Mountbatten," Harkness, U.K., 1983; "Lavender Dream," Interplant, Holland, 1984; "Modern Art," Poulsen, Denmark, 1984; "Artiste," Dorieux, France, 1984; "Bordure Rose," "Bordure Vive" and "Bordure d'Or," Delbard, France, 1979–85; "Matthias Meilland," Meilland, France, 1985.

Uses of Cluster-Flowered Roses

In discussing Large-Flowered roses (roses tending to be single-flowered) we advised against cutting so as to retain their full decorative effect in garden displays; and such restraint is even more necessary in the case of the Cluster-Flowered roses, which

43

Page 43: "Conrad Ferdinand Meyer," a vigorous upright shrub with large, highly scented pink flowers.
Page 45: "Pink Grootendorst," notable for its resemblance to a carnation.

bloom, like the Large-Flowered types, at the tips of the stems but, as their name indicates, in clusters.

Certain points must be borne in mind: there are many more flowers than are produced by single-flower varieties, the size of the corollas is generally smaller, and the clusters do not all bloom simultaneously—the central flowers open before those on the outside, so it is best to purchase the varieties whose flower petals drop naturally as they fade. Before making a definite choice for the garden it is advisable to pay several visits to parks, public gardens or nurseries with representative displays. Varieties are usually labeled and nursery catalogs provide essential information.

Floribundas are typically used to create large patches of color, but the especially sturdy varieties are also excellent for ornamental hedges (e.g., in ascending order of height, "Masquerade," multicolored, "La Sevillana," red, and "Iceberg," white). In a small garden effective patches of color can be obtained by planting at least three bushes of the same variety, but not in straight lines. The best display, however, comes from six or nine plants arranged in a double circle with one in the middle, or in a square of three rows.

To enliven a limited space even further, the bush in the center can be replaced by a standard; this is a rose formed of a young straight stem generally of a Rugosa variety, grafted, about 1.5 m. (5 ft.) high, with another, cultivated variety. In a medium-sized garden it is a good idea to use even taller standards of pendulous habit (there are two forms, one umbrella-shaped, the other weeping, i.e. hanging down the stem). These can lend the garden a romantic note and are, in any event, eye-catching examples of ornamentation used less nowadays than in the past.

Bush Roses

Although by definition all roses are classified as bushes, i.e. woody plants with many close branches arising from or near the ground, in practice bush roses are those of erect habit and less vigorous than those known as shrub roses. Bush roses are those usually used for bedding, for which shrub roses are not suitable, because of their greater size or their informal habit of growth.

One Japanese species, *R. rugosa*, has provided many shrub roses either directly or with progeny created by hybridization with other species. Flowers of *R. rugosa* appear in oriental paintings of one thousand years ago; and in 1784 the species was described by the German botanist Thunberg, followed a dozen or so years later by the first specimens to reach Europe. However, only toward the end of the nineteenth century were there serious attempts at breeding. Its typical attributes are recurrent flowering, the characteristically wrinkled foliage, vigor, resistance to intense

cold and adaptability even to sandy soil; such qualities opened up enticing possibilities of mingling with the positive features of other species.

"Blanc Double de Coubert," with white, double, flattened and scented flowers, was among the first varieties (1892) and was followed a few years later by "Conrad Ferdinand Meyer." From Haÿ-les-Roses came "Rose à Parfum de l'Haÿ" and the even more fragrant "Roseraie de l'Haÿ." Other excellent varieties made their appearance over the years, and just before World War II "Scabrosa" was discovered, having previously escaped attention, at the Harkness nurseries in England; it has mauve-red flowers, large, single and highly perfumed, and like other varieties of R. rugosa shuns warm, dry climates as well as clay and chalk soils. When flowering is over it produces large numbers of fleshy, decorative hips, characteristic of the species.

Also belonging to the Rugosas are the so-called carnation-roses ("Fimbriata," "F.J. Grootendorst," "Pink Grootendorst").

Obviously not all roses of shrubby habit have R. rugosa as their ancestor. With apologies for inevitable omissions, here is a list of representative shub roses of other origins.

The botanical species include R. chinensis mutabilis, R. eacae, R. foetida, R. gallica x macrantha, R. hugonis, R. moyesii, R. roxburghii and R. sericea (many of which are described and illustrated in the plates). In addition there are "Golden Wings"*

* Description and illustration in Plates section.

Below: "Priscilla Burton," one of McGredy's so-called "hand-painted"
roses.
Bottom: "Rush," recently raised by the Belgian Louis Lens.

and "Stanwell Perpetual"* (hybrids of *R. spinosissima*), "Canary Bird" and "Golden Chersonese" (descended from *R. xanthina*), "Wilhelm"* (derived from *R. moschata*), "Centenaire de Lourdes"* (with "Frau Karl Druschki" as mother), "Nevada"* (regarded as progeny of *R. moyesii*), the multicolored "Joseph's Coat"* and the recent "Mountbatten"* from Harkness.

Hand-painted Roses

In 1971 a certificate of merit from the Royal National Rose Society was awarded to the variety "Picasso," which had attracted the attention of the judges because of the unusual color arrangement of its semi-double flowers. The upper side of the petals was cherry-red irregularly streaked on a white ground, and the reverse side was also white. Sam McGredy, who created it, called it a "hand-painted rose," and this felicitous name was thereafter used to distinguish varieties with similar features produced by the same breeder; these gradually displayed some variations of color, a large number of petals, more decorative foliage, a greater abundance of flower clusters, recurrence and vigor.

Here, in chronological order, is the brief list of Cluster-Flowered hand-painted roses so far produced; they already represent an important advance in rose breeding, but doubtless there will be further developments, unpredictable at this stage, in this specialized field. A few of the varieties are "Old Master" (1974), "Matangi" (1974), "Eye Paint" (1976), "Priscilla Burton" (1978) and "Regensberg" (1979). In 1984 a variety from Dickson in Northern Ireland, "Dikerry," was awarded a gold medal in the demanding selective trials of the Royal National Rose Society. The semi-double flowers are quite large; there is an irregular white patch in the center of the corolla, and the crinkly edges of the petal are bright pink.

Roses of Yesterday and Today

Between 1936 and 1937 three very similar varieties of rose were unexpectedly introduced to the public. They were all free-flowering and recurrent, of dense and vigorous growth, about 1.5 m. (5 ft.) in height, with tight clusters of small, single flowers in various shades of pink with a white patch in the center.

The first two varieties, named "Ballerina" and "Belinda," both with delicate pink and white-eyed flowers, were introduced by the Essex (U.K.) firm of J.A. Bentall. The third, "Mozart," apparently related to the others but with deeper pink flowers, came from the German breeder Peter Lambert.

These prototypes of a new race were exceptionally vigorous, with balanced growth and an abundance of flowers over a long period—ideal for decorative effect in the garden (midway between shrub roses and the typical bush varieties). In recent years this type of rose seems to have been rediscovered and its potentialities recognized. Harkness is one of the breeders who has shown interest. "Yesterday" (1974) attracted much attention, its growth slightly untidy but with delicate sprays of small, narrow-petaled, fragrant flowers, lilac-pink with a silver center; and in 1977 he introduced "Marjorie Fair," described as a copy of "Ballerina," with carmine, white-eyed flowers.

The Belgian breeder Louis Lens appears to have taken matters a step further with "Rush" (1983). This variety has a semi-rounded habit and bears dense clusters of pink flowers which are bigger than those mentioned above; if given drastic pruning in winter it makes a compact shrub—in which case the plants should be set 60 cm. (24 in.) apart; pruning at longer intervals will produce plants up to 1.5 m. (5 ft.) in height and width.

This new race of vigorous Modern Polyanthas, very recurrent and less prone to disease than the earlier varieties, will probably be used increasingly to provide gardens with a uniform display of brilliant five-petaled blooms, to form groups or to create a compact patch of color in or around a lawn.

Ground Cover Roses

For some years there has been growing interest in trailing or ground cover roses, characterized by long shoots that tend to spread more or less horizontally and can be used for filling beds placed at high level and spots not easily accessible, either hanging down or to form broad masses of color. In addition to their ornamental value they can often be useful in checking the spread of weeds in areas devoted to roses.

The branches stretch out actually on the surface or just above it. They are usually planted in groups (one or two to the square meter, according to their vigor) in well-prepared ground generously treated with a slow-acting fertilizer such as bone and hoof meal. This provides nutritive elements suitable for roses destined for a long stay in one position—an important consideration given that their growth habit may prevent the easy application of fresh fertilizer.

Some natural botanical species (nonrecurrent) have a ground-covering habit, as for example R. wichuraiana and the related R. luciae; in their country of origin, Japan, both are used to great decorative effect—with their lovely glossy foliage—on sloping sites, particularly along river banks. The common Field Rose (R. arvensis) also has long trailing stems which it has passed on to R. x paulii (hybrid of R. arvensis x R. rugosa) and its beautiful variety R. x p. rosea. The very long, thin stems—up to 5 m. (17 ft.)—with their single flowers, white in the type species, seem to attract masses of butterflies when in bloom, a delightful sight which unfortunately lasts for only a few weeks. In the garden R. x paulii and its pink variety need stakes, fixed at a height of about 25 cm. (10 in.), to support the loose stems, which can be trained like the

spokes of an enormous wheel. Staking is also necessary for horticultural varieties of *R. wichuraiana*, listed in catalogs as ramblers, although their dense tangle of branches will hardly lend themselves to such geometrical patterns.

In 1919, when nobody yet thought of using ground cover roses in the garden, a hybrid of *R. wichuraiana* x *R. rugosa*, possessing such attributes, was introduced in the United States. It was called "Max Graf" and is regarded as the prototype of this new style of rose. Its dense branches, over 1 m. (3 ft.) long, keep down weeds and root as they make contact with the soil, creating patches of color on slopes and exposed sites. "Max Graf" can withstand the coldest winters and is not prone to disease; it has leathery leaves and bears single bright pink flowers with a yellow center. A spontaneously produced species from it (*R. kordesii*) was used by the German breeder Wilhelm Kordes to produce a group of extremely vigorous roses, resistant to hard frosts and diseases, with a climbing habit and a single, long flowering period.

Recent introductions have included "Rote Max Graf" and "Weisse Max Graf," with single red and white flowers respectively, branches 2 m. (6 ft.) long and persistent foliage through the winter; these characteristics are also present in "Heidekönigin" and "Repandia." All are varieties raised by Kordes.

Other recent ground cover varieties include "Sea Foam" (Schwarz, U.S.A., 1964), with small shiny leaves and double, clustered white flowers, awarded the gold medal in the 1964 Concorso Internazionale in Rome; "Nozomi" (Onodera, Japan,

How to train climbing shoots for best flowering results (Coggiatti's climbing Hybrid Tea "Mon Amour").

1968), almost a Miniature with bright single mother-of-pearl pink flowers; "Snow Ballet" (Clayworth, New Zealand, 1977), with white double flowers; the vigorous "Fair Play" and "Pink Star" (Interplant, Holland, 1977), red and deep pink respectively, followed recently by "Rosy Carpet," with single carmine-pink flowers.

Each year sees an increase in available varieties. In 1979 Sam McGredy sent to Europe his "Snow Carpet," a Miniature ground cover rose with double white flowers; and then it was the turn of Louis Lens, with the more vigorous "Pink Spray," "White Spray," "Running Maid" and "Tapis Volant," followed by Poulsen with "Pink Bells" and "Red Bells." And the firm of Meilland foresees that the answer to numerous problems of use and maintenance, both for private and public clients, will be provided by a wide range of roses that differ in appearance and habit, marketed under the names "Meidiland" and "Meillandécor."

Since relatively few summer-flowering varieties are available, Meilland are aiming to produce and select roses to fill this gap, initially with an eye to mass planting. But the diverse habits of the roses belonging to this group encourage various uses; broadly speaking, there are three growth categories:

1) roses with a trailing habit;
2) roses with an upright, then drooping habit;
3) roses with dense branches and upright habit (2–3 per sq.m.).

Intermediate forms of these types make possible a multitude of landscaping effects, since they bear large numbers of flowers of long duration, the plants are very vigorous, they can be propagated by cuttings (encouraging branching from the base and elimination of suckers), and they are resistant to the hardest frosts and to diseases. Not the least of the qualities is the splendid panoramic effect of large groups all flowering together.

A varied selection of Meilland varieties would include: "Swany," with glossy foliage, trailing or drooping habit, flat double flowers, recurrent; "Pink Meidiland," erect habit, large leathery leaves, big clusters of single pink flowers, recurrent; "Ferdy," upright then drooping branches, 70–90 cm. (28–36 in.) long, with tight bunches of small pink double flowers; and "La Sevillana," vigorous shrub with dense growth right from the base, free-flowering and recurrent, clusters of scarlet flowers.

Climbing Roses

References in *The History of Plants* by Theophrastus and in Pliny's *Historia Naturalis* enable us to identify at least two roses of ancient times with very long branches; they appear to belong to the species nowadays named *R. canina*, the Dog Rose or Briar (known to the ancients as *Cynorrhodon*), and *R. sempervirens* (*Coroniola*); others that could be added are *R. arvensis* and *R. moschata*, even though both appear not to have been known to the classical authors of agricultural literature that has come down to us. Yet none of these species was among those grown in gardens of the time. It is worth remembering that the name *R. canina* is based on that given by the Greeks (Dioscorides) and the Romans (Pliny), implicitly referring to the use of its root as a cure for hydrophobia.

R. sempervirens, with its evergreen foliage, is one of the many plants cultivated in antiquity to furnish material for fashioning the wreaths worn by guests at elaborate banquets. The first reports concerning the progeny of *R. sempervirens* destined for garden ornamentation date from 1826 and 1827, and refer to two beautiful varieties with small evergreen leaves and fragrant, flat, double white flowers, blooming in late spring. These two varieties were obtained in France by Louis Philippe's gardener; the first was dedicated to the king's daughter and called "Adelaide d'Orléans," the other was named "Felicité et Perpétue," possibly after the gardener's own daughters.

R. arvensis is notable for its long stems which in nature are trailing and entangled, so much so that it might well be included among the modern ground cover roses rather than the climbers.

R. moschata, a very vigorous species with branches up to 6 m. (20 ft.) long, is variously believed to have originated either in Central Asia or in southern Europe, and flowers in late summer and autumn. The specific name *moschata* derives from the scent given out by its flowers (particularly from the pollen-bearing

51

anthers), comparable to the secretions from the scent glands of the musk deer (*Moschus moschiferus*), and is in no way associated with moss.

R. moschata played an important role in the early years of the nineteenth century; it was the first rose from the West which, fertilized with pollen from one of the recently introduced recurrent Chinese varieties, transmitted this attribute to progeny of the second generation which became the parent stock of a new type of recurrent and, in large measure, climbing rose. This race took the name of *R. noisettiana* after the American grower (of French origin) Philippe Noisette, who concluded the breeding work begun by John Champeney of Charleston.

Botanists in the past made no special mention of roses with a climbing habit, and the inference must be that they had no place in the garden. Centuries elapsed before climbing roses assumed a more important role, particularly as an ideal means of covering ample areas of fence and wall.

Somewhat earlier, there were references to two varieties of climbers descended from the ancient *R. sempervirens* which were the first known to have been used in gardens; these were *R. multiflora carnea* and *R. m. platyphylla*, both of which had reached Europe from Japan. In the introduction of roses from Asia, the original species was often preceded by its varieties, and these two, like the initial progeny of *R. chinensis*, *R. odorata*, *R. banksiae* and *R. wichuraiana,** are the best-known examples. The reason this seems to have happened so frequently is probably that the varieties were much more numerous, so that the few travelers from Europe who were allowed into China and Japan brought back to the Old World those that appeared most worthwhile.

About seventy years ago almost all the climbing roses were derived from plants which had been obtained from seeds of the *polyantha* and *wichuraiana* varieties or, more rarely, from other sources such as *R. x anemonoides* (a descendant of *R. laevigata*), "Mermaid," a hybrid of *R. bracteata*, and (mild climate permitting) hybrids of *R. banksiae*, *R. odorata* (Teas) and *R. noisettiana* ("*Gloire de Dijon*,") "*Maréchal Niel*," etc.). These varieties were flexible enough to be used for covering pillars or for shaping into chains and garlands, typical decorative features of the day.

A good deal later, the previously mentioned ground cover variety "Max Graf" was raised. From this came *R. kordesii* and the long list of Kordes climbers, starting with "Hamburger Phoenix" and "Leverkusen." Many are recurrent, unlike the once-flowering group of sturdy, frost-resistant roses previously raised by the same breeder from crosses with various forms of *R. pimpinellifolia*; even today, after almost fifty years, there is

---

* Detailed descriptions in relevant Plates.

"Miami Holiday," from Ralph Moore (California), who specializes in growing Miniature Roses.

widespread admiration for two extremely vigorous varieties, 2.5 m. (8 ft.) tall, "Frühlingsgold" (1937), with fragrant golden-yellow flowers, and "Frühlingsmorgen" (1941), with enormous, single cherry-pink flowers.

At this point it might be helpful to distinguish between a climber and a rambler. Both have long shoots and climb or scramble over and up things, and although their thorns give some purchase they do need to be tied if used on an arch, pergola or fence. A climber has quite big flowers in small trusses and forms a permanent framework of rather stiff canes. In pruning only the side shoots should be cut back by about two-thirds. A rambler has large clusters of small flowers and, unlike many climbers, is nonrecurrent. The shoots are flexible and new ones come up from the base each year. For pruning, cut away completely the shoots that have flowered as soon as this is over and tie the new shoots in their place.

Sports

Rose varieties with a complex lineage sometimes tend to produce mutations commonly known as "sports;" these involve the structure of the chromosomes and the cells, sometimes altering the morphology of the plants themselves.

Even scientists do not know what factors induce a mutation and can only make assumptions, but the possible consequences are plain to see. The following are among the alterations in appearance and habit that may occur in roses: change of petal color or change of variegated petals to single-toned petals, or vice versa; loss of thorniness; acquisition of recurrence; acquisition or loss of mossiness; consistent increase or decrease in number of petals; transformation from shrubby to climbing habit. This last permutation is most frequent in Hybrid Teas and Floribundas, and it manifests itself in the elongation of a branch which does not stop growing at its customary height. This will supply material for propagation (by grafting, cutting or layering) which will produce a rose with the attributes of the mutated branch. In some cases there may be reversion to a shrub, caused by overdrastic pruning or, in roses that are not too vigorous, by the ineffectiveness of the shoot (basal or apical) used for propagation.

During the present century there has been a tendency for climbing varieties that are sports of bush roses to become predominant. Because the other characteristics usually remain unaltered (except for recurrence, which is markedly reduced), the two forms, though retaining the same varietal name, are distinguished by the initial "Cl." to denote the climber, as for example "Peace" and "Cl. Peace," "Queen Elizabeth" and "Cl. Queen Elizabeth," "Iceberg" and "Cl. Iceberg," etc.

After some years the stems of the climbing varieties become thicker and stiffer, and it is advisable to plant such roses with their branches spread out fanwise against a supporting wall or trellis to increase flowering.

Roses of any type will do best if grown in sunny positions. In zones with very high summer temperatures, climbers against walls that are likely to become too hot should not be allowed to come into direct contact with the surface but trained on wires a little distance from it, to improve air circulation.

Pruning

Because climbing roses need to be pruned in a very different manner from bush or shrub roses, a brief note on this procedure is essential. Nonrecurrent ramblers, generally hybrids of *R. wichuraiana*, should be pruned at the conclusion of flowering with the elimination (not merely shortening) of old wood. This thinning-out encourages the growth of new branches which can become woody before the frosts.

Miniature Roses

In the early years of the eighteenth century a few roses with miniature flowers were already being grown in Europe, among them "Pompon de Bourgogne," still found in a few gardens. However, these old varieties were far bigger than the tiny Miniature roses raised today. Furthermore, the flowering period of the older types was very short, lasting a mere two to three weeks.

John Lindley, author of *Rosarum Monographia*, published in 1820, states that the catalog of the botanical garden on the island of Mauritius listed a *R. pusilla*, identifiable as the so-called *R. lawrenceana* which Robert Sweet, before 1820, had brought back to England from that island (although it was commonly believed to have originated in China). Pierre Joseph Redouté, in his imposing trilogy on roses (1817–24), almost certainly illustrates the same rose under the name *R. indica pumila*, together with the French name "Rosier nain du Bengale;" but both the terms *indica* and "du Bengale" are incorrect. This "Bengal rose" was so named simply because ships carrying Chinese roses back to Europe rested them for a while in Calcutta Botanical Gardens so that they could survive the long journey by sailing ship. When this rose arrived in the West it was assumed that it originated in Bengal. Actually it was a descendant of the ancient *R. chinensis* (*R. c. minima*), hence the same *R. pusilla* as had come to England from Mauritius. In the first half of the nineteenth century the progeny of this rose became established as the nucleus of the new family of recurrent Miniatures; among the earliest and most famous of these was "Pompon de Paris," others being "Caprice des Dames" and "Miss Lawrence's Rose."

In 1917—almost a century after the arrival in Europe of *R. c. minima*—Doctor Roulet, a Swiss army medical officer, noticed on the windowsills of several houses in the mountain village of Onnens (Swiss Juras) pots containing tiny roses which, according to the owners, had been grown there for years. The botanist Henri Correvon considered it to be a new species and named it *R. rouletii* after its "discoverer," failing to compare it with "Pompon de Paris," from which it differed only in small details. Because of this similarity, *R. rouletii* and "Pompon de Paris" are regarded by many as synonymous.

The so-called *R. rouletii* had the effect of awakening people's interest in Miniature roses at a time when rose breeding had developed into a professional and widely practiced activity. So while the first descendants of *R. c. minima* were probably sports or the products of self-fertilized seeds, two dedicated and skilled breeders (the Dutchman Jan de Vink and the Spaniard Pedro Dot) used *R. rouletii* for raising new hybrid varieties. The former crossed it with "Cécile Brunner" and various other Polyanthas, while Pedro Dot used one of his own Hybrid Teas as well as "Cécile Brunner."

Miniatures of Yesterday and Today

For fifteen years Jan de Vink and Pedro Dot were the only professionals engaged in raising Miniatures, obtaining excellent varieties, some of which are still grown successfully today. The most interesting introduced between 1940 and 1950 were, from Pedro Dot, "Estrelita de Oro" ("Baby Gold Star"), "Rosina" ("Josephine Wheatcroft"), "Para Ti" ("Pour Toi"), "Perla de

Alcanada" and "Perla de Monserrat;" and from Jan de Vink, "Tom Thumb" ("Peon"), "Pixie," "Midget," "Sweet Fairy," "Cinderella" and "Bo Peep."

In due course they were joined by the American Ralph S. Moore, who made profitable use of his own experience and that of his precursors to obtain, among many other types, new Miniature varieties, verifying that it was sufficient for only one of the parents to belong to this category. The following is a short list of varieties raised by Moore, in four selected groups:

New colors: "Lavender Lace," lavender-mauve perfumed flowers; "Green Diamond," small light green flowers.

Mossiness: "Kara Moore" and "Dresden Doll," both with pink flowers, sepals, calyx and stem covered with scented moss.

Variegated petals: "Over the Rainbow," bicolored yellow-red flowers; "Magic Carrousel," white flowers with red borders.

Climbing forms: "Pink Cameo" (1954), described by Moore as the first recurrent climbing Miniature;* "Red Cascade" (1976), also used for ground cover or for trailing over a wall.

The example set by Dot and de Vink was followed by a number of leading European growers, notably Meilland (whose "Starina"

---

* Evidently Ralph Moore's claim refers to the varieties which, though climbers, maintain the reduced plant size as well as the minimum dimensions of leaves and flowers. In fact, floriferousness and recurrence (at the unlikeliest times, either before or after the normal flowering period) are features of the climbing sport of the shrub variety "Pompon de Paris," 2 m. (6½ ft.) in height, which has been cultivated for many years.

Another climber, very recurrent and also extremely vigorous, is "Cl. Cécile Brunner;" this too, in spite of its extraordinary vigor, retains unaltered the small flowers and leaves.

and "Darling Flame" were placed first and second in the Royal National Rose Society's table of Miniatures). Other famous varieties from European growers included "Zwergkönig" (1978) and "Zwergkönigin" (1982) from Kordes; the veteran "Baby Masquerade" from Tantau; "Mini-Poul," with flowers of changing hues, "Bluenette" and "Blue Peter," both lavender-blue, from Poulsen; and the recent "Dorola," "Angelita" and "Little Artiste" from McGredy in New Zealand.

Along with ground cover varieties designed for the large garden, there are now smaller roses in the same class with flowers as tiny as those of Sam McGredy's appropriately named "Snow Carpet." There is steadily growing interest in such roses, and the same could be said for what might be called the "intermediates," officially known as Dwarf Cluster-Flowered. They are halfway between the Miniatures and normal-sized Cluster-Flowered roses and include modern varieties such as "Wishing," "Anna Ford," "Dainty Dinah" and "Robin Redbreast."

In fact, however, these halfway roses are by no means new, and many of the old Polyanthas could be included among them. With a few exceptions, these fell from favor many years ago with the coming of the more vigorous Floribundas (which were their direct descendants), but a few of the best have survived. Even earlier there were roses like the dwarf Centifolia "Pompon de Bourgogne"—dating from the eighteenth century, with fragrant, double pink flowers—but toward the end of the nineteenth century two superb Polyantha varieties were introduced in France

which, by virtue of their elegance and recurrence, attracted an enormous following and still have many enthusiastic admirers: "Cécile Brunner" and "Perle d'Or." The latter has small double apricot-yellow flowers, perfumed and perfectly shaped, and pointed glossy leaves; in the right soil and with favourable climatic conditions it forms a dense bush 1.5 m. (5 ft.) high. "Cécile Brunner" is a captivating little rose, its flowers light pink and more strongly scented than those of "Perle d'Or." "Cécile Brunner" comes in three forms: all retain the same beautifully shaped small flowers and deep green leaves, but they have different habits of growth. The original plant does not exceed 40 cm. (16 in.) in height, the shrub form (sometimes known as "Spray Cécile Brunner," sometimes as "Bloomfield Abundance") grows to human height or more.

As stated above, given satisfactory climatic conditions, soil and light, "Perle d'Or" as an adult becomes a dense, strongly growing bush. So here are two typical examples of roses which can grow to a considerable size while retaining small flowers and leaves.

Some years ago Louis Lens, the Belgian grower and breeder who raised that wonderful variety "Pascali," tried to generate interest in the subject of Miniatures outgrowing their normal size with an article in the magazine *Les Amis des Roses*, with wholehearted backing from the then president of the Société Française des Roses, Armand Souzy. He cited many examples of Miniature roses which, in particularly favorable surroundings,

could reach a height of some 80 cm. (32 in.) while displaying the original unchanged attributes of small flowers, stems and leaves.

"Meillandina"

For some years the firm of Meilland has raised and distributed a new race of dwarf roses of compact habit and with an abundance of double, medium to small flowers, named "Meillandina." As a rule, three young plants obtained from cuttings and grown in the same small pot are offered for sale, already in flower, at the end of winter. Buyers can keep the plants for some weeks on the windowsill or in some other cool but very bright spot. When this first flowering period is over the plants can be transferred to the balcony or planted out in the garden.

The "Meillandina" family comprises many varieties with brilliant colors ranging from orange, red, yellow and apricot to pure white and white streaked with red.

Other breeders are working along similar lines; particular mention should be made of the Dutch firm de Ruiter, with "Rosamini" and "Minimo."

Use of Miniature Roses

After alternate periods of popularity and eclipse, Miniature roses have, over the last few decades, come back into their own.

In the garden a row of Miniature roses, uniform in size and shade, can make an effective border to a small bed, enliven a rockery or provide a solid and lasting patch of color to contrast with the lawn. Alternatively, a couple of plants can fill spaces in the paving of a terrace or patio. On the balcony, single plants can be set in small pots or several specimens (preferably of the same variety) in larger pots adequate for their eventual growth.

Cultivation

Miniature roses planted in the open need a mixture of good garden soil and a compound fertilizer with all the main nutritive elements. For containers special preparations are available that include phosphorus, potassium, iron, a small quantity of nitrogen and trace elements. A supply of natural, dehydrated manure reduces the need for chemical fertilizer.

Watering—reduced but not suspended in winter, frequent and plentiful in summer—should be sufficient to prevent the soil drying out completely. Water should not be allowed to stand for long periods in the pot-holder.

As with other roses, Miniatures require continuous light in order to flower properly, preferably in a sunny spot for much of the day; they may be harmed by long periods of hard frost.

Pruning

Pruning, though simplified, differs little from that for larger bushes. The branches can be shortened to achieve balanced growth, and in any case it is necessary to cut off dead wood at the base or remove any branch which shows excessive vigor, especially if it is thrusting upward. Thin or tangled twigs should also be removed. A plant that has suffered long neglect may be revived by severe pruning, which will encourage young growth and give a chance for new shoots to develop.

INTERNATIONAL ROSE TRIALS

The first international trial organized to draw up a graded list of new roses offered by the trade was held in June 1907 at Bagatelle, just outside Paris.

Since 1958 another kind of trial has been held at Orléans, the French rose-growing capital; here awards are given to recurrent forms of bush, Cluster-Flowered and climbing varieties that have been available to the public for five years and which exhibit attributes indispensable to international success: vigor, decora-

tive foliage, resistance to disease, shape and color of flowers, etc.

Lyons, the city which was the birthplace of such famous growers as Pernet-Ducher, Guillot, Meilland, Gaujard, etc., instituted trials in 1926 to award an annual prize to the loveliest rose in France. And from 1978 the Société Française des Roses has given new impetus to exhibitors by organizing, in addition to existing trials, an annual international competition which awards the title of "Grandes Roses du Siècle" to five roses of each type, a prize for perfume and designation "Selectionnée par la Société Française des Roses" to other worthy novelties.

Italy was the second European nation to establish an international competition for new roses, mainly with a vew to finding the most suitable varieties for hot, dry summer conditions. The Associazione Italiana della Rosa has gained international recognition and the beautiful garden where the competitions are held contains a wide range of interesting varieties. Other trials are held at Monza and, since the autumn of 1985, at Genoa-Nervi. Awards are given to the best new roses from Italy and abroad, in all classes and for the usual attributes, including perfume.

Geneva's magnificent rose collection in the Parc La Grange, comprising some 12,000 plants of 180 varieties, was established in part to alleviate Switzerland's unemployment problem after World War II. The city authorities, with an eye to tourist attraction, called upon all the available unemployed to create the garden, which in due course became the venue for international trials for new roses.

The variety "Chrysler Imperial" provides a splendid mass of color, the dark red flowers, flushed with an even deeper shade, contrasting magnificently with the dark green foliage.

In the Federal Republic of Germany the annual trials for new roses are held at Baden Baden, a delightful spa town which attracts many tourists. There is also a rigorous selective trial (Anerkannte Deutsche Rose) to assess new varieties (mostly German) divided into all the main categories and judged on a regional basis.

Madrid's Rosaleda is perhaps the most spectacular of all the European rose gardens, situated across from the Parque de l'Oeste and named after its founder, Ramon Ortiz Ferré.

Belgium holds two famous international competitions, one at Courtrai (Kortrijk) in western Flanders, the other at Le Roeulx in Hainault, both in beautiful surroundings close to well-known castles. The former competition is held early in July and the latter, to emphasize recurrent varieties, in mid-September.

Holland's impressive Westbroekpark lies halfway between The Hague and the seaside resort of Scheveningen. Well separated groups of roses are planted in clearings surrounded by ancient trees; and a suitable area is reserved for the international trials which since 1962 have held three separate competitions for new roses, existing roses and highly perfumed roses.

The Royal National Rose Society of the United Kingdom, which vies with the American Rose Society for symbolic pride of place, has its offices in St Albans, near London. There is a twelve-acre rose garden and adjacent trial grounds where roses are judged over three years by a process quite different from that employed in the rest of Europe; a national jury of sixteen experts judges the roses entered. Another trial is held in Belfast, Northern Ireland, where prizes are awarded for the best Large-Flowered, Cluster-Flowered and perfumed varieties.

The international competition organized by the city of Dublin, Eire, highlights Miniature roses in addition to the traditional forms.

In the United States one or two new roses are declared winners of the All-America Rose Selection. After two years of controlled cultivation in eight different trial grounds situated in states with very different climates, the coveted AARS seal is awarded.

Other selective competitions, organized along similar lines to those already mentioned, are held in Japan, New Zealand, Australia and other countries.

CLIMATE, SOIL, LIGHT AND PLANTING

Zones with moderate atmospheric humidity, intermittent rainfall and winter temperatures that do not drop below about $-12°$ C ($10°$ F) are nevertheless preferable to others. Theoretically, the ideal soil for growing roses is one with—preferably—a moderately acid to moderately alkaline chemical reaction, with some clay, well drained and reasonably exposed to the sun. If plants can be bought from a nearby nursery, it is advisable to choose roses which have been propagated from rootstock that has proved well suited to the local soil and climate. Here are some examples of the characteristic habits of certain types of rootstock:

R. canina: withstands frost; suffers as a result of high alkalinity and long summer drought.

R. indica major: can stand drought thanks to deep roots; does well in chalky soil; dislikes hard frosts.

R. laxa: also does well in chalky soil. The least prone to sucker.

R. multiflora: does well in acid soils; very extensive root system.

R. rugosa: adaptable to sandy, peaty and wet soils; withstands low temperatures.

It has to be added that the rootstock is not always a guarantee that the grafted plant will do well.

Except in places where summer sun is excessively hot, roses enjoy the maximum amount of light. Lack of light causes branches to become thin, flowers to diminish in size and fewer buds to form at the tip of the branches; there may be other reasons for these failings (atmospheric or soil pollution, fluctuations in temperature, etc.) but they are certainly consequences of a shady site.

A rose should ideally remain for a number of years in the position where it was planted; it has to feed leaves and flowers and must form a good number of strong branches, hence the need for careful preparation of the soil in which it is set.

If a dozen or so bush roses are to be planted in a group, there are two alternative procedures: a) single holes measuring not less than 40 × 40 × 40 cm. (16 × 16 × 16 in.); b) digging and preparation of trenches likewise 40 cm. (16 in.) deep. The distance between plants will depend on the vigor of the variety concerned and the effect to be achieved (Cluster-Flowered for masses of color or single-flowered for individual beauty), and will thus vary from 35 to 70 cm. (14 to 28 in.). A lesser distance is required for Miniatures. Roses planted to provide a hedge need deeper and wider holes or trenches. In the case of only a few, isolated roses, whether bush or climbing varieties, it is best to plant them in single holes leaving 15–20 cm. (6–8 in.) more than the distances suggested above.

Whatever the method of planting, care must be taken to mix the lowest layer of soil with a slow-acting organic fertilizer such as bone meal or hoof meal. Halfway down, but not in contact with the roots, some fresh or dehydrated manure can be added; finally, about 50 g. (2 oz.) of a chemical fertilizer with all the basic nutritive elements (nitrogen, phosphorus, potassium and iron) and possibly an addition of some trace elements (manganese, boron, etc.) should be mixed in with the surface layer. Before planting, the roots should be well spread out and the soil sprinkled into the gaps without leaving air pockets. After planting, the soil around the plants should be lightly pressed down and then well watered.

Black spot can be controlled reasonably well by immediate treatment with a good fungicide.

Pruning

The traditional pruning months in the United Kingdom are March in the south and April in the north, when the bushes will just be ending their dormancy. Delay the pruning, however, if there is frost about, as this is likely to cause newly cut shoots to die back. In the United States, hard pruning is done annually in early spring just as plants are ending their dormancy.

Apart from encouraging new growth, the reasons for pruning are: to get rid of dead, diseased and spindly shoots (any much less than pencil thickness); to open out the center of the bush to promote air circulation; to end up with a reasonably balanced bush. Pruning is most easily done with pruning shears or secateurs. Make your cuts just above a bud and at an angle of about 45°, sloping down away from the bud.

With Large-Flowered (Hybrid Tea) roses—once the dead and diseased wood has been removed and the bush center opened up—the remaining shoots should be pruned back to 15–20 cm. (6–8 in.) If you can, cut to a bud that faces in the direction in which you wish the new shoot to grow. With Cluster-Flowered (Floribunda) roses the same sequence is followed, but the main shoots can be left rather longer—say 25–30 cm. (10–12 in.)—with their side shoots shortened by about two-thirds. Shrub roses that grow like giant Cluster-Flowered varieties should have their height reduced by about two-thirds, and most old garden roses need their side shoots cut back by about the same proportion. Wild

Below left: caterpillars are busy in the spring.
Below right: aphids infest young leaves and buds.
Bottom: rose chafers mainly damage white or pale-colored roses.

(species) roses need only dead wood removed.

Autumn pruning means cutting the taller bedding roses back by about one half to prevent the winter winds rocking them about too wildly and loosening them in the soil. This cutting is done late when the plants have lost most of their leaves. Stems that are cut back will need to be shortened further in the following spring.

Propagation

After many decades when budding has been by far the commonest method of propagation with professional growers, there are signs that it is on the decline.

Micropropagation, which makes use of tiny pieces of plant tissue rather than buds and means that thousands rather than perhaps ten new roses can be produced from a single bush, is rapidly revolutionizing rose growing. The plants are produced in laboratories rather than the field, the pieces of rose tissue rooted in test tubes, but although major rose growers are already using this method, not all are convinced that it will produce plants with the vigor and longevity of those grown on rootstocks in the traditional way. Suckers would, however, be a thing of the past.

The average gardener cannot, of course, even contemplate carrying out micropropagation and most are daunted by the thought of attempting budding which does require a certain dexterity, not to mention the extra work of growing the rootstocks. If you feel you do not want to tackle this, you can increase your roses by taking cuttings. These will not increase the number of varieties in your garden but will simply add to what you already have unless you take the cuttings from elsewhere— perhaps the garden of a friend who has varieties you would like.

While you can use a greenhouse or cold frame, rose cuttings will root quite successfully in the open in very mild climates. The best time to take them is late summer or early autumn. Use fully ripe shoots of the current season's growth.

The cuttings should be grown in an open, airy spot with some shelter from the midday sun. If your soil is heavy, dig a narrow trench 15 cm. (6 in.) deep and sprinkle a little coarse sand along the bottom to help in rooting. In light soil, make a slit 15 cm. (6 in.) deep by pushing a spade in and working it back and forth.

Your cuttings should be 23 cm. (9 in.) long, the bottom cut being made just below a bud and the top cut just above one. Remove the thorns but leave the top pair of leaves. Whether you use a hormone rooting powder is up to you. If you have dug a trench, put your cuttings vertically along one side of it 15 cm. (6 in.) apart. When you have filled in the trench, 15 cm. (6 in.) of each cutting should be below ground. If you have merely made a slit, insert the cuttings to the same depth and tread the soil firm. Over winter the cuttings should root and in spring new shoots will appear. Do not move them until a full year has passed.

Diseases and pests

Black spot. Rounded black spots with fringed edges appearing first on the lower, older leaves, usually from July onward. Spray with benomyl or triforine. Burn affected leaves.

Canker. Canker spores enter through a wound in a shoot, forming brown, cracked areas. Cut away shoot below canker.

Caterpillars. Irregular holes eaten in leaves. Remove by hand or spray with fenitrothion, gamma BHC (HCH) or permethrin.

Chafers. Beetles, large and small, which nibble rose petals. Spray with fenitrothion or gamma BHC (HCH).

Froghopper. Blobs of froth where leaves join shoots are the signs. Froghoppers—pale yellowish-green, sap-sucking insects—hide in these. Pick off by hand or spray as for greenfly.

Greenfly. Small green or sometimes pink insects which cluster on rose shoots and leaves, sucking the sap. Any insecticide will deal with these. Systemic insecticides (and fungicides) remain active longer than others, as they penetrate the plant tissue and so are not washed off by rain. Systemic insecticides are dimethoate and heptenophos.

Japanese beetles. Handsome, 1-cm./½-in. metallic-colored beetles are attracted by the color of the flowers, and they chew the flowers and leaves to pieces. Spray with carbaryl as necessary or pick off by hand into can of kerosene.

Leaf-rolling sawfly. Adult females lay their eggs in leaf margins and at the same time inject a toxin which causes the leaf to roll up lengthwise, protecting the grub when it hatches inside. Only preventive spraying in late April with fenitrothion is effective.

Mildew. White powdery-looking coating on leaves and flower stems, spreading quickly. Spray with benomyl or triforine, so the same spray will deal with both black and mildew.

Red spider mite. Minute animals which suck sap from the undersides of the leaves, usually troublesome only in the open garden in hot dry weather. Very difficult to control, but they do not like water. Dimethoate (systemic) spray may sometimes help.

Rose rust. Not common everywhere. Orange spots on undersides of leaves, which later turn black. Spray with oxycarbon or propiconazole.

There are a few other pests that may cause minor damage such as rose leaf miner, rose slug worms and thrips, all of which can be dealt with in one go with a systemic insecticide.

General rules for spraying

Always wear rubber gloves when handling chemicals. If there is any wind at all, always spray downwind so that the spray vapor will blow away from you. Do not spray in hot sunshine or you may scorch the leaves. Early morning or evening is best. Always follow the instructions on the bottle or packet when preparing sprays.

1   ROSA X ALBA "INCARNATA"

Synonym "Cuisse de Nymphe," "Cuisse de Nymphe émue," "Great Maiden's Blush," "Maiden's Blush."

Origin Natural hybrid after the sixteenth century; the original species still grows naturally in some parts of Europe, but is probably no longer cultivated.

Description There are two forms, both taller than 1 m. (3 ft.), nonrecurrent and with scented petals; broadly speaking, one of them is more vigorous, with slightly bigger flowers with pink tints; the other ("Cuisse de Nymphe"="Maiden's Blush") with soft pink petals, almost thornless stems and more numerous leaflets (normally seven not five). Apart from their undeniable beauty, the lasting popularity of these roses is in part due to the suggestiveness of their French and English names. Other old varieties: *R. x a. maxima, R. x a. semi-plena.*

Use Collectors' gardens. Noted for perfume and characteristic spring flowers.

☐ *Plates 1–27 represent botanical species and first-generation descendants.*

2   ROSA X ANEMONOIDES

Synonym "Anemone Rose," "Anemonoides."

Origin *R. laevigata* x (variety of) *R. odorata*, hybrid species obtained in 1895 by J.C. Schmidt, rose grower from Erfurt, Germany.

Description Climber, quite decorative during brief flowering period; single flowers, early blooming, large (10 cm.–4 in.), soft pink, slightly scented, nonrecurrent or insignificantly so in late autumn. Small, sparse, glossy dark green leaves, with three, sometimes five leaflets. In areas with harsh winters it needs a sunny position and protection from cold winds. In 1913, in California, the sport "Ramona" appeared, notable for its more deeply colored petals.

Use Pergolas and trellises.

3 ROSA BANKSIAE "ALBA-PLENA"

Synonym *R. b. banksiae.*
Origin Certain varieties of *R. banksiae* arrived in Europe before the original species; this particular variety was the first to be introduced to England from Canada in 1807. There is mention of a specimen of the original species arriving in Scotland from China in 1796, but it never flowered there because of the cold winter climate; a cutting sent to the owner of a garden in Nice subsequently flowered in 1909. However, it is recorded (on the basis of specimens on show at the international exhibition held in Florence in 1874) that the three specimens of *R. banksiae* with single flowers were obtained from seeds unexpectedly furnished by the *alba-plena* variety.
Description Climbing rose which in temperate-warm climates, a couple of years after planting, grows branches over 10 m. (33 ft.) long, generally without thorns. It flowers once, in spring, and is extraordinarily prolific, with violet-scented blooms.
Use Pergolas and walls and covering trees with tall trunks. Easily propagated by cuttings in autumn.

---

4 ROSA BANKSIAE LUTEA

Synonym "Banksian Yellow."
Origin Variety introduced to England in 1824 by John Parks, who was sent to China by the Royal Horticultural Society to collect new plants.
Description Double flowers, very numerous after period of acclimatization, medium-small, pale yellow; very interesting although less fragrant than *alba-plena*. Has the customary vigor of the species, and is regarded as the least susceptible to frost. There is another variety with single creamy yellow flowers, highly perfumed (*R. b. lutescens*), introduced to Europe after *lutea*, testifying to the large number of natural and cultivated varieties to be found in China.
Use As for *alba-plena* variety.

5   ROSA BANKSIAE NORMALIS

Synonym *R. banksiae*, regarded as the true species.

Origin The specific name commemorates Lady Banks, wife of the director of Kew Gardens, vice-president of the first directive council of the Royal Horticultural Society, and botanical explorer (1793–1820). During the last decades of the nineteenth century various European botanists (Regel, Delavay, Poatanin and A. Henry) came across it in China, but it is hard to say which of them introduced it to Europe, and in which year. It is widely distributed in its natural state in various regions of China (Shensi, Kansu, Hupeh, Szechwan and Yunnan), growing at different latitudes; this is probably why it varies in appearance and number of leaflets (sometimes with, but also without, down), in the presence or absence of thorns, in the number of flowers to each cluster, etc.

Description Single flowers, rounded, white, highly scented. Customary vigor of species; climbing shoots green and not much branched, foliage semi-persistent in mild climates; single, early flowering; sensitive to hard, lasting frosts.

Use As for *alba-plena* variety.

---

6   ROSA X CENTIFOLIA

Origin Described for the first time by Clusius (Charles de l'Écluse) in *Rariorum Plantarum Historia* (1601); he named it *R. c. batavica* (after its presumed Dutch origin) to distinguish it from the ancient rose of that name, which was considered lost. It is probably the natural "fixed" hybrid of *R. damascena semperflorens* and *R. alba*. It was widely portrayed by Flemish artists.

Description Averagely vigorous bush with open habit; the branches are prickly, with hooked thorns. Flowers scented, double (*centifolia* = with a hundred petals), pink. The excessive number of petals has been at the expense of reproductive organs, so that *R. centifolia* is sterile and is propagated by cuttings. One prolonged flowering period in spring.

Use Collectors' gardens; short hedges supported by galvanized iron wire and special stakes.

7 ROSA X CENTIFOLIA "CRISTATA"

Synonym "Chapeau de Napoléon"
Origin In the Prévost Fils catalog of 1829 it is said of this rose: "I have been told this is of Swiss origin ..."
Description In the words of the catalog: "Of the sepals surrounding the corolla, two are long on both edges, and a third only on one edge; the appendages, in many parts, are subdivided into little short, straight strips, with many very small scent glands. It would be wrong to think that the extraordinary calyx of this rose resembles that of the so-called Moss roses." The buds, when still closed, have the characteristic appearance that has given the rose its French name.
Use Collector's rose.

8 ROSA X CENTIFOLIA "MUSCOSA"

Synonyms "Common Moss," "Communis," "Old Pink Moss"
Origin A sport of *R. centifolia* which appeared somewhere in Europe in the early years of the eighteenth century; first reports of it go back to 1720.
Description This variety differs from the species in having a spongy, scented plant tissue, looking like moss and covering calyx, stalk and young growth. Leaves and corolla are slightly smaller, but the pink color and perfume of the flowers are the same as for the species. It is regarded as the loveliest of the Moss roses. To prevent mildew, it is essential to make sure that there is plenty of air by removing superfluous or weak branches after flowering.
Use Collector's rose; groups of not more than three plants.

9 ROSA CHINENSIS

Synonyms "China Rose," *R. bengalensis*, "Bengal Rose"
Origin The original species, doubtfully identified in 1884 by the botanist Henry growing wild in the Hupeh valley, China, does not exist in cultivated form. From the end of the eighteenth century different varieties, the result of mutations and selections that had taken place over the centuries in Chinese gardens, were introduced into Europe. Among the most representative were *R. c. pallida*="Pink China"="Old Blush," and *R. c. semperflorens* ="Slater's Crimson China." The former originated from *R. x noisettiana* (=*R. c. pallida* x *R. moschata*) and from *R. x borboniana* as a result of crosses with *R. damascena semperflorens*. The seeds obtained by crosses with *R. chinensis* gave the bright red petal color to the progeny.
Description Shrubs of moderate height; leaves (3–5 leaflets) slightly thorny, often mahogany-red when young; branches thin with sparse thorns. *R. c. pallida* is found in gardens devoted to old roses; much rarer is *R. c. semperflorens*, known in two forms, one of which—reintroduced to Britain in 1957—is about 1 m. (3 ft.) high and has flowers with few petals; the other with dark red double flowers. It was the varieties of *R. chinensis* which first transmitted the recurrent attribute to Western roses.
Use Collector's rose.

10 ROSA CHINENSIS "MUTABILIS"

Synonyms *R. mutabilis*, "Mutabilis," "Tipo Ideale"
Origin In the late nineteenth century this rose, the name and origin of which were unknown, was much admired in gardens on the shores of Lake Maggiore. The Swiss botanist Correvon tentatively described it as a new species, calling it *R. mutabilis*, a name subsequently corrected by Rehder to *R. chinensis mutabilis*.
Description A bush with open, spreading habit; in temperate zones the branches (initially mahogany-red) reach a height of 1.5 m. (4–5 ft.)—2.5 m. (8 ft.) if grown up a wall. The large, single, fragrant flowers are the rose's principal attraction and account for its specific name, because the buds are orange-red, then change to pink and then, as they open, to purple-red. The plant is very free-flowering and recurrent.
Use Single specimen, free hedge.

11 ROSA CHINENSIS "VIRIDIFLORA"

Synonyms *R. viridiflora*, *R. monstruosa*, "Green Rose"
Origin A probable sport of a china rose; grown for a century and a half, perhaps longer.
Description A rose famous for the singular color and appearance of its flowers, which lack scent; the greenish petals with a touch of reddish-brown are dense in the center of narrow green segments derived from the transformation of stamens and stigmas, and have a leafy appearance.
Use Can be grown in the garden, but as a botanical curiosity rather than for ornamental purposes.

12 ROSA DAMASCENA "TRIGINTIPETALA"

Synonym "Kazanlik"
Origin It is difficult now to trace the original Damask species. It was probably descended from a natural cross at some distant time past between *R. gallica* (from Europe and the Middle East) and *R. phoenicia* (from the Near East); another cross, between *R. gallica* and *R. moschata* (originally from the Mediterranean basin) may have given rise to the variety which flowers frugally in autumn, though named "Semperflorens" or, less misleadingly, *R. bifera*. The offspring of this second crossing may be Virgil's "Rose of Paestum." In spite of the name, it is doubtful whether it comes from Damascus, and it is equally doubtful whether it was introduced to Europe by the Crusaders, as is sometimes maintained.
Description The highly fragrant, nonrecurrent *R. d. trigintipetala* (with thirty petals), widely cultivated in the Kazanlik valley of Bulgaria is used to extract the essence known as Attar of Roses. The old variety *R. d. versicolor* has a bushy habit with long, flexible branches; flowering once a year, its petals are white with light red streaks or splashes, for which reason it is called the "York and Lancaster Rose," as if to mark the reconciliation of the two warring houses.
Use Collector's rose.

13 ROSA FOETIDA

Synonym *R. lutea* (pre-Linnean name), "Austrian Yellow"
Origin Southwest Asia; possibly a sport of *R. haemispherica* (illustrated in main text). References to its cultivation in Europe date from the sixteenth century, but it is probably a much more distant introduction.
Description Large numbers of single flowers, cup-shaped, bright yellow and with a disagreeable scent, bloom the length of slender branches, up to 2.5 m. (8 ft.) or even longer; the smell and the tendency of the leaves to be attacked by black spot have prejudiced growers against this rose which, when in flower, is extremely decorative. In the sport *R. f. bicolor* ("Austrian Copper")—illustrated—the flowers take on a red color in the upper part of the petal and, although they sometimes revert to the original yellow, this produces a pleasing contrast. It is, in fact, the first example of a bicolored rose. According to W.F. Bean, this mutation was already familiar in the Arab world in the twelfth century.
Use Worth featuring with plenty of space around it.

14 ROSA FOETIDA "PERSIANA"

Synonym "Persian Yellow"
Origin Southwest Asia; introduced to Britain at the beginning of the nineteenth century. Probably a sport of *R. foetida*.
Description A vigorous bush with showy golden-yellow flowers in spring, sprouting shoots from the root. It is advisable to grow nongrafted specimens. *R. f. persiana* has played an important role in the evolution of the genus *Rosa*, and the Lyons rose grower Joseph Pernet-Ducher finally succeeded, just before 1900, in using its pollen to fertilize a Hybrid Perpetual, obtaining the first modest variety of what was to become the famous class of roses known as Pernetianas. This transmitted to its offspring not only the golden-yellow color of the parent but also the varied red tonalities derived from *R. f. bicolor*. The Pernetianas were later widely crossed with Hybrid Teas and eventually merged with them.
Use A very decorative bush when in flower; a milestone in the history of roses.

15 ROSA GALLICA

Synonym *R. rubra*
Origin Eastern France, western Italy, central Europe across to western Asia.
Description This is the oldest species of the genus *Rosa* in the West, ancestor of the majority of modern roses. Some rose experts dispute the statement that the original species possessed only five-petaled flowers; because of the possibly uninterrupted cultivation of the species through the centuries, this is nowadays hard to determine. The height of the bush varies from 50 to 120 cm. (20 to 48 in.); the root system produces runners and suckers. Leaves have 3 to 5 leaflets, thorny on the lower side; flowers are generally bright pink, perfumed. For some six centuries the most widely grown and popular variety has been *R. g. officinalis*, sometimes called "Apothecary's Rose." From the thirteenth century, in fact, the pharmacists of Provins (a town in the Île de France, south of Paris) specialized in the preparation of powders, confections and syrups from the highly fragrant petals of the rose; this industry, over the years, brought so much prestige and fame to the town that the common name in France today is "Rose de Provins" (illustrated here).
Use Collector's rose, not only for its historical interest but also for its beauty and the scent of the flowers.

16 ROSA GALLICA "VERSICOLOR"

Synonym "Rosa Mundi"
Origin A sport, with variegated petals, of *R. gallica officinalis*. It is mentioned in a text of 1581 and is therefore the oldest variegated rose.
Description Apart from the white streaks, bands or patches on the petals, it is identical to the variety from which it is derived, with branches about 70 cm. (28 in.) long, showing a few scattered thorns, and semi-double, very fragrant flowers; it is very prone to mildew. There is a tradition that the name "Rosa Mundi" is associated with the Fair Rosamund, mistress of the English king Henry II (twelfth century).
Use Decorative in the garden, despite its short flowering period and its predisposition to mildew.

17 ROSA GALLICA X R. MACRANTHA

Synonym "Complicata"
Origin So far it has not been possible to discover anything about its ancestry. In the lists of the historic garden of Haÿ les Roses it is described as an interspecific hybrid, as it is for the purposes of our own listing.
Description A very vigorous shrub with spreading habit and slightly curved outer branches; grows to 2.5 m. (8 ft.) if supported by another shrub. The branches are plentifully covered with single, very large pink flowers of about 12 cm. (5 in.) diameter, initially cup-shaped, then flat. Quite beautiful during its long flowering period.
Use As mentioned above or as free hedge (very effective if space permits).

18 ROSA HUGONIS

Origin A Chinese species introduced to England in 1902 and dedicated to the Rev. Hugh Scallan, who had sent its seeds to Kew Gardens.
Description The upright or curving branches grow to a height of 2.5 m. (8 ft.) and to about the same breadth; it blooms once, very early, the flowers being single, about 5 cm. (2 in.) across, with bright primrose-yellow petals, and studded the length of the branches. Some interesting forms with five-petaled yellow flowers and large thorns have been derived from this species; these are usually considered to be the result of natural crosses with *R. sericea pteracantha* and "Canary Bird" (and perhaps *R. hugonis* x *R. xanthina spontanea*—see entry on later species); these also bear very early single yellow flowers.
Use Preferably as isolated specimens. Propagation by cutting is better than by grafting; this and excessive wetness of the ground may cause collapse of plants, in the case of both *R. hugonis* and "Canary Bird."

19 ROSA LAEVIGATA

Synonyms *R. sinica*, *R. triphylla*, "Cherokee Rose"
Origin Southern China, Taiwan, naturalized in Georgia and other southern states of the United States, where its common name of "Cherokee Rose" is derived from the Indian tribe of that name.
Description The long dark leaves have, almost always, three leaflets with characteristic threadlike stipules at the base. The flowers are single, 8–10 cm. (3–4 in.) across, white and perfumed; the sepals are covered with dense, short hairs. One flowering period in spring. Does not withstand persistent frosts. There is a hybrid species, *R. x anemonoides*.
Use Ideal for covering the trunk of a tree or for climbing a fence or trellis.

---

20 ROSA MOSCHATA

Synonym "Musk Rose"
Origin Reputedly indigenous to the Mediterranean region and western Asia, but nowadays not to be found growing wild (W.J. Bean). Judging from the cytological research carried out by Dr. C.C. Hurst, it appears probable that a remote wild cross with *R. gallica* resulted in the recurrent *R. damascena semperflorens* (*R. d. bifera*); furthermore, artificial hybridization, probably with *R. chinensis pallida*, led to the appearance of the Bourbons and thus to the Hybrid Perpetuals and many modern varieties.
Description The specific name is derived from the scent emitted by the anthers, similar to that given out by the gland of the musk deer *Moschus moschiferus*, a rare component of expensive perfumes. Botanically it belongs to the group of so-called Synstylae (with styles fused in a column), like the related *R. brunonii*, which used to be known as *R. moschata nepalensis*. It is a fairly free-growing climber, usually with single white or cream flowers, although semi-double and double forms are known. In the past, because there were no recurrent roses, *R. moschata* was valued for its late flowering period (August onward).
Use Merits a place in the botanical history of the rose for its part in the evolution of the genus *Rosa*.

21 ROSA MOYESII

Origin A species introduced in Europe in 1903 by E.H. Wilson and dedicated to the missionary J. Moyes, who gave hospitality and help to the plant-seeker at the turn of the century.

Description A vigorous bush, 3–4 m. (10–13 ft.) high with curving branches at the top; compound leaves (up to 13 leaflets) and single, velvety petaled flowers in variable tones of crimson (late spring), followed later by bright, decorative hips. The variety "Geranium" (illustrated here), raised in 1938 by the Royal Horticultural Society, is notable for its slightly more compact growth, the brilliant color of its flowers and the beautifully shaped and very numerous orange-scarlet hips.

Use On its own or with other flowering shrub varieties, preferably yellow ones, as for example *R. ecae*, "Canary Bird" and "Golden Chersonese."

---

22 ROSA MULTIFLORA

Synonym *R. polyantha*

Origin Japan and Korea. Back in 1784 the botanist Carl Peter Thunberg had already discovered, described and named this rose in his *Flora Japonica* under its present valid botanical name. It was subsequently "rediscovered" by the botanists Siebold and Zuccarini who, unaware of the previous denomination and description, called it *R. polyantha*; the rose became popular by this name, although it was not officially recognized. In due course hybrids of *R. multiflora* and varieties of *R. chinensis* produced what came to be known as Polyantha roses.

Description A tall shrub with arching branches, 4–5 m. (13–16 ft.) long, leaves dull green, consisting of 7 to 9 leaflets; dense panicles of single white flowers, about 2 cm. (¾ in.) diameter, scented.

Use As rootstock, generally for acidic soils where, often outliving the budded variety, it will grow vigorously and give a fine show during its brief flowering period. One thornless form is used along highways in the United States at dangerous junctions. As a collector's rose, it has ornamental value.

23 ROSA RUBRIFOLIA

Synonyms *R. glauca, R. ferruginea*
Origin In dry clearings of mountain woods, at altitudes of 500–1500 m. (1,650–5,000 ft.), of central and southern Europe.
Description Upright habit with shoots sprouting from base, about 2.5 m. (8 ft.) high, branches reddish or purple like the leaves, which are initially lighter, bluish-purple. There are many small flowers, sometimes five or more single blooms in a bunch. After flowering, small red hips appear, giving the bush a decorative appeal.
Use Flowers, foliage and branches are attractive and unmistakable. The cut branches are often used for indoor arrangements.

24 ROSA SEMPERVIRENS

Origin Mediterranean region. Although the earliest written records go back to 1561 (Anguillara), it is assumed that it was known in Roman times.
Description A vigorous climbing rose with a habit midway between a trailer and a rambler, with branches up to 6 m. (20 ft.) long. Single white flowers, growing individually or in bunches of up to five. The glossy leaves last even through the winter (hence the specific name, which in translation is "evergreen"); this is a recessive trait in the genus *Rosa* which could be of interest to breeders. It cannot withstand long and severe frosts, but some of the very few hybrids are hardier, particularly the rambler "Félicité et Perpétue" of 1827.
Use As a collector's item, in climates that are not too harsh.

25 ROSA SERICEA

Synonym *R. omeiensis*
Origin Northern India, Burma and central Asia. It exhibits differences according to place of origin, some of little significance (var. *R. s. omeiensis*, originally from the Omei Mountains of central China), others of considerable interest (*R. s. pteracantha*, with huge winged thorns, the variety illustrated here).
Description The major interest for the gardener is perhaps the unusual flower which, as a rule, has only four petals, a unique feature that would alone justify its inclusion in any garden scheme. White is the normal petal color, but shades of cream and sulphur-yellow are also regarded as valid, since these are found in specimens originating from different localities (Bean). The bush is vigorous with an upright habit, 2–3 m. (6½–10 ft.), with single, isolated, unscented small flowers, diameter 3–4 cm. (1¼–1½ in.), which bloom once, early.
Use Of considerable botanical interest, because of its four petals and the large decorative thorns of the variety *R. s. pteracantha*.

26 ROSA WATSONIANA

Synonyms *R. multiflora watsoniana*, "Bamboo Rose"
Origin Introduced to the United States from Japan before 1870; apparently never found in its wild state.
Description In the past it was described as a variety of *R. multiflora*, then restored to the species status given it by Crespin and today agreed as such by Bean; in *Modern Roses 8* it is said that propagation by seed produces roses of the normal *R. multiflora*, but this statement is contradicted by Shepherd (*History of the Rose*), who nevertheless confirms its affinity with the latter. The bush has flexible branches and benefits from a suitable support; in spring it produces delicate pyramidal inflorescences of small white or pink flowers. The feature that gives the rose curiosity value is the foliage; the leaves are formed of 3 to 5 narrow, ribbonlike leaflets, ½ cm. (¼ in.) wide and almost 10 cm. (4 in.) long, with wavy, not toothed margins. This characteristic foliage has earned it the popular name of "Bamboo Rose."
Use Its interest is mainly in the very peculiar design of the leaves, which can make it a focal point of the garden from May to autumn, despite the short flowering period.

27 ROSA XANTHINA SPONTANEA

Origin *R. xanthina* has double flowers, a peculiarity which has caused puzzlement about its true botanical identity. There are indications that it may have originated from a seed of *R. x. spontanea* accidentally pollinated by a different rose. Jack Harkness, in his book *Roses*, suggests that the varietal name "Canary Bird" is, in most cases, applicable to *R. x. spontanea*.

Description A large, attractive bush about 2 m. (6½ ft.) tall, with long brown branches which tend to droop, arching at the tip. The small, soft leaves make a pleasing background to the many bright, early-blooming flowers, which are scented and look like little golden-yellow bells.

Use Should not be grown where there are long harsh frosts, in ground exposed to too much sun or in poor soil. Thrives on plenty of fertilizer applied at time of planting. Can be featured as an isolated specimen or as a free hedge.

---

28 TUSCANY   ○

Origin This has been identified as the Velvet Rose included in a list of fourteen roses described in John Gerard's *Herball* of 1596. "Tuscany Superb" (illustrated here), commercially available since the middle of the nineteenth century, is regarded as its seedling (N. Young) or as one of its forms (J. Harkness).

Description More upright in habit and less thorny than other varieties of *R. gallica*; notable for the dark, velvety crimson-maroon color of its semi-double, flat, slightly scented flowers. The petals of "Tuscany Superb" are larger, more numerous and more velvety, and the leaves are rounder.

Use Occupies an important place in any collection of old roses. It is advisable to remove or drastically shorten older branches at the end of the single flowering period in late spring.

○ *Plates 28–60 represent bush and shrub roses up to 1910.*

29 KÖNIGIN VON DÄNEMARK

Synonym "Queen of Denmark"
Origin Authoritative sources differ as to when this rose was introduced (1809, 1816, 1826) and where it came from (Denmark, Germany, England); see, in this context, G.S. Thomas, *The Old Shrub Roses*. It is uncertain whether it belongs to the Alba group, as claimed by some authors; nor is there universal agreement as to the beauty of the flower as compared with "Mme Hardy" and "Duc de Guiche," its great contemporaries.
Description The exquisite shape of the buds, the deep carmine-pink color of the flower as it opens and the subsequent delicate flesh-pink of the petals, allied with the strong fragrance, made this one of the most popular roses of the nineteenth century. Growth is healthy and vigorous, although less upright and more open than other varieties of *R. alba*. This suggests a possible link with *R. damascena*.
Use In a collection of old roses. Does well in a position that is shady for part of the day.

30 CAMAÏEUX

Origin A variety of *R. gallica* with variegated petals, introduced in 1830, probably in France; not even the grower's name can with any certainty be determined. The name "Camaïeux" comes from Arabic, the original meaning being "flower buds," but later "hard stone in different colors."
Description A less vigorous rose than other descendants of *R. gallica*, about 1.2 m. (4 ft.) tall and some 70 cm. (28 in.) across, and needing a more fertile soil; compensating for all this are the unpredictable semi-double flowers which, when they open, are pink with stripes or streaks in red, crimson and purple; subsequently purple tends to predominate. Deeply perfumed. It is more refined, though less spectacular, than *R. gallica versicolor* ("Rosa Mundi"), and the petal shades tend to be somewhat variable.
Use A curiosity for the rose collector.

31 ROSE DES PEINTRES

Synonym "Centfeuilles des Peintres"
Origin This rose is described, without mention of the grower, in the Prévost et Fils Catalog of 1829. It is thought to be a sport of *R. centifolia* or a hybrid, *R. centifolia* x *R. gallica*.
Description A sturdy rose with dark green, deeply toothed leaves; flowers large and rounded, with close, excellently shaped, scented petals. There is one long flowering period. It is one of the so-called Cabbage roses. Often portrayed by the Flemish painters, it has closed buds and the fringed sepals characteristic of many Centifolias.
Use A collector's rose, useful for cut flowers in period arrangements.

32 DUC DE GUICHE

Synonym "Sénat Romain"
Origin A variety of *R. gallica* which features in the catalog of roses cultivated by Prévost et Fils of Rouen (1829), with no indication as to who raised it; it was presumably Prévost himself.
Description The catalog states: "Branches large and stiff; leaflets oblong and very pointed. Flowers very big, double, lilac-pink, taking on a lilac-gray tone in very high temperatures." G.S. Thomas places this variety on a par with two of his favorite roses, "Mme Hardy" and "Belle de Crécy;" a judgment we share. Max Singer's *Dictionnaire des Roses* (1885), and that of Simon and Cochet (1906) both agree on the violet-red color of the petals. The rose reaches 1–1.5 m. (3–5 ft.), with one early to normal flowering period; it is perfumed.
Use In collections of old roses.

33 MME HARDY

Origin A variety of *R. damascena*, with *R. centifolia* as another probable ancestor. It was introduced in 1832 by Eugène Hardy (then curator of the Jardin du Luxembourg in Paris), who dedicated it to his wife.
Description The most admired and coveted of all old roses, a prize possession in any garden. In fertile soil it can easily reach 2 m. (5–6 ft.); its growth is somewhat ungainly but tends to be fairly upright; the soft light green leaves are prone to mildew in badly ventilated positions. These are insignificant drawbacks, fully compensated for by the astonishing beauty of the perfumed flowers at the tips of the lateral branches; the unique design of the corolla cannot adequately be described, but may perhaps be compared to a delicate cup of fine porcelain in whose gentle curve innumerable white petals seem to describe concentric circles, gradually decreasing to surround a tiny central green emerald.
Use Group grown on its own; cut flowers.

34 FANTIN LATOUR

Origin Some fifty years ago Graham Stuart Thomas, that champion of the unrivaled beauty of old roses, discovered in an English garden a fascinating, vigorous but anonymous old rose (apparently closely related to the Centifolias), simply labeled "the loveliest rose in the garden." True though this may have been, the name was not confirmed by the discoverer.
Description The great French painter Fantin Latour (1836–1904) left valuable pictorial evidence of many roses of his day; the unknown English variety, with corollas resembling "his roses," was dedicated to him as a spontaneous expression of well-deserved gratitude. G.S. Thomas, though recognizing its affinity with the Centifolias by the shape of the flowers and their nonrecurrence, saw in the shiny leaves a link, too, with *R. chinensis*.
Use Individual specimens or small groups; cut flowers.

35 FÉLICITÉ PARMENTIER

Origin A rose cultivated since 1834; raiser unknown.

Description The bush grows to a maximum height of 1.5 m. (5 ft.); the leaves are light green, with a lesser tendency to blue, and the branches are more open than is usual among other descendants of *R. alba*, suggesting a possible relationship with *R. damascena*. The rounded, creamy-yellow buds develop, in late spring and early summer, into almost spherical many-petaled flowers, soft, delicate pink and strongly scented. The branches tend to bend under their weight and superfluous buds should be removed.

Use When planting, the distance between individual plants should be carefully measured to allow for the open habit of the branches.

---

36 STANWELL PERPETUAL

Origin Probably *R. damascena semperflorens* x *R. spinosissima*, a seedling which appeared as a wild sport in a garden of the English village of Stanwell and was introduced in 1838 by the nurseryman Mr Lee.

Description In fertile soil it grows like a large shrub, being almost 1.5 m. (5 ft.) tall and equally wide, with a rather untidy habit. It is therefore advisable to plant a few specimens close to one another, for reciprocal support. The branches—as attested by the specific name of the male parent—are very thorny, the small leaves are an interesting gray-green, and the perfumed flowers, flat and double, are abundant during the first early period and then diminish until the autumn, when rain may prevent them opening.

Use As single specimens, given suitable support. The cut flowers show off the pale pink and then white of the petals and the unusual color of the leaves.

37 CARDINAL DE RICHELIEU

Origin A variety of *R. gallica* attributed to the Frenchman Laffay (1840) who, according to statistics concerning the growers and breeders of the nineteenth century, had to his credit some 388 roses. Other authors say that this variety came originally from Holland under the name "Rose Van Sian."

Description The green, almost thornless branches are upright in habit and reach 1.2–1.5 m. (4–5 ft.). The large flowers, from rounded buds, have a triple corona of purple-violet petals, almost white at the base, and are surrounded by other, larger petals curving toward the outside of the corolla. G.S. Thomas's supposition that *R. chinensis* appears in the family tree of this variety is sustained not only by the glossy leaves but also by the need—unusual in *R. gallica* varieties—for the soil to be carefully worked at time of planting so that it is fertile and not dry.

Use In groups, as part of a collection.

---

38 CHARLES DE MILLS

Origin Written information about this rose is scarce and confused. Neither its parentage nor its date of birth is known: Norman Young, in *The Complete Rosarium*, suggests that the raiser was a certain Desportes, active between 1800 and 1835 and better known as author of *Rosetum Gallicum* published in Le Mans in 1828. This individual is not listed among the 175 "principal raisers of roses" in Simon and Cochet's *Nomenclature de tous les noms de roses*, published some time afterward. Furthermore, a rose under the name "Bizarre Triomphant," a synonym of the present variety, appears in this book as no. 1542 of a list of 11,000 names, and is described as a violet-gray variety of the Bengal Rose (i.e. *R. chinensis*), whereas "Charles de Mills" is without any doubt a variety of *R. gallica*.

Description A rose with open habit, vigorous, 1.3–1.5 m. (4–5 ft.) tall, with sparse thorns; the stocky buds open into many flowers with flat corollas, full of short, fragrant petals in a succession of red tonalities; the buds seem to have been sliced in half with a very sharp blade.

Use Very interesting during its six weeks of flowering, when it needs some support. Deserves a prominent position.

39 SOUVENIR DE LA MALMAISON

Origin A cross ("Mme Desprez," a Bourbon with lilac-pink flowers x an otherwise unidentified Tea rose with yellow petals) made by Jean Beluze of Lyons shortly before 1843. The Grand Duke of Russia, during a visit to the garden of Malmaison, admired the unnamed rose, took away a specimen and requested that it be called "Souvenir de la Malmaison."

Description It is considered the most successful variety of Bourbon rose, the class which played a determinant role in the creation of the Hybrid Perpetuals, which later joined ranks with the Hybrid Teas. In mild climates it will grow to more than 2 m. (6½ ft.) and has to be kept under control by careful pruning. Persistent rain can spoil the flowers whose beauty, otherwise, is considered unsurpassed. The size of the blooms, the regular arrangement of the many petals, the pale blush-white color, the marked recurrence and the penetrating scent are the chief characteristics of this very fine variety. The climbing form is nonrecurrent; L.A. Wyatt warns that this should be noted at time of buying, to avoid disappointment.

Use The fact that flowers are almost continuously present between the two main flowering periods makes it especially useful in the garden.

40 BELLE DE CRÉCY

Origin Although there is wide agreement on the name of the raiser (the French grower Roeser of Crécy en Brie), there is no such consensus about the lady who inspired the name, or on the date when this variety of *R. gallica* appeared. Norman Young, in *The Complete Rosarium*, places it between 1830 and 1836, G.S. Thomas (*The Old Shrub Roses*) before 1848, and M. Gault and P.M. Synge (*The Dictionary of Roses*) before 1848, probably in the early 1800s. Léon Simon (*Nomenclature de tous les noms de roses*) omits its date, although he mentions those of nearly all the other 11,000 roses. As for the dedication, it has been interpreted as the "beautiful rose of Crécy," but some attribute the epithet "belle" to the Marquise de Pompadour, who had lived some seventy years before at the castle of Crécy.

Description A bush of medium height with virtually thornless branches and mainly open habit; it benefits from a couple of supporting stakes and close contact with other roses. Its beauty is at its peak during the three-week flowering period, when it is considered unrivaled for its many double, perfumed flowers, beautifully shaped and gradually becoming flatter, as if the petals were setting out to reveal their intricate arrangement.

Use In a group, alongside other low-shooting, upright varieties of *R. gallica*, such as "Tuscany Superb" and *R. g. officinalis*.

41 GLOIRE DES MOUSSEUX

Synonyms "Gloire des Mousseuses," "Madame Alboni"
Origin A variety of *R. centifolia muscosa*, probably raised by Laffay of Bellevue-Sèvres in 1852.
Description The attribution of the title "glory of Moss roses" to this admittedly remarkable variety may be disputed. Nevertheless, at least along the stalk and sepals there is an abundance of scented moss which, with the shapely light green leaves, highlights the showy double, deep pink flowers with the characteristic Centifolia fragrance.
Use Growing to little more than 1 m. (3 ft.), it should not be hidden by other more vigorous plants.

42 SALET

Origin A variety of *R. centifolia muscosa* raised by the Lyons grower François Lacharme in 1854.
Description Although there are only modest quantities of moss on the sepals, stalk and hips, the compensation is a long period of recurrence. The pleasing pink flowers tend to fade at the edges and are scented; this becomes more pronounced in the evening. The bush, which reaches a height of 1.2 m. (4 ft.), has green branches, a few long thorns and many smaller thorns; the light green leaves are also prickly. Edward A. Bunyard, who in 1936, was among the first growers to draw attention to old roses, considered "Salet" to be "one of the best."
Use For flower arrangements with other Moss roses.

43 REINE DES VIOLETTES

Origin Cataloged as a Hybrid Perpetual inasmuch as it is thought to be a seedling of "Pius IX," which has very similar flowers. Nevertheless, the shape of the flowers (in their initial phase) resembles that of the Bourbons or Gallicas. Raised in France, marketed since 1860.

Description A vigorous, low-shooting bush which will grow to 1.5 m. (5 ft.) in fertile soil and with hard pruning in winter; if cultivation is neglected, however, plants will be short-lived. Sparse gray-green foliage, thin flower stems with a characteristic leaf which appears just below the corolla. The flowers deserve their vernacular name: 70 short petals initially form a sort of cup, deep violet in color; the corolla then flattens and in the next few days a pale red flush appears. The first flowering is abundant and prolonged; the flowers continue, in lesser numbers, until autumn. They are strongly, sharply perfumed.

Use Each specimen needs plenty of space around it.

44 LA FRANCE

Origin A cross between a Hybrid Perpetual and a Tea, tentatively suggested as "Mme Victor Verdier" x "Mme Bravy," raised by Jean-Baptiste Guillot, son of the founder of the celebrated rose-growing firm of Lyons.

Description A committee of fifty growers assembled at Lyons in June 1867 to judge more than a thousand new varieties raised in France, and voted that this one should bear the name "La France," considering it even to represent a new class of rose. Thus appeared the first Hybrid Tea variety with elegant leaves, slender flower stems and whorled flowers, heralding the end of the era of Hybrid Perpetuals. After a confused period of uncertainty Hybrid Teas established themselves all over the world, but the modest direct descendants of "La France" played no part in this, despite having pointed the way to crosses between the vigorous, perfumed Hybrid Perpetuals and the gentle, recurrent Teas.

Use Deserves to be represented in any rose collection.

45 PAUL NEYRON

Origin Antoine Levet of Lyons, who raised this variety in 1869, dedicated it to his young friend Paul Neyron, who was to be killed the following year in the Franco–Prussian War. It was a Hybrid Perpetual, derived from a cross between two varieties of the same class ("Victor Verdier" x "Anna de Diesbach").

Description A very vigorous shrub which grows to human height, free-flowering and recurrent. The very large, globular, double flowers, 12–13 cm. (4¾–5¼ in.) in diameter, pink with a lilac flush and slightly scented, grow from the tip of long, solid stems bearing broad, glossy foliage. It was enthusiastically received both in gardens and florists' windows; for many years the "Neyron pink color," then new, was all the rage in the high-fashion dressmaking salons.

Use For collections of historical roses; cut flowers for period arrangements.

46 MME PIERRE OGER

Origin Derived as a color sport from "La Reine Victoria" (a Bourbon variety). It is widely agreed that "Mme Pierre Oger" is superior to its maternal parent. The sport appeared, during the years before its introduction in 1878, in the nurseries of the grower A. Oger of Caen in northern France.

Description It is distinguished from the parent variety by the very delicate, pale mother-of-pearl pink of the petals, which seems even softer under a cloudy sky. The slender, upright branches, reaching a height of up to 2 m. (6½ ft.) bear globular flowers, often four or more on a single stem, with perfumed, shell-shaped petals. The flowers are most abundant in the two main flowering periods (end of spring and beginning of autumn) and appear sporadically in the interim. It is best to apply preventive treatment against mildew in spring and against black spot in late summer.

Use Make a wonderful display in a group together with related species "La Reine Victoria" and "Louise Odier."

47 GÉNÉRAL SCHABLIKINE

Origin A Tea rose raised in 1878 by the grower Gilbert Nabonnand, oldest of the family of rose breeders active on the French Côte d'Azur until the early years of the present century.
Description A vigorous shrub with scattered large thorns on the branches; the mahogany red of the young leaves indicates the presence of *R. chinensis* among its antecedents. The first very early and abundant flowering period is followed by two more; the flowers, single or in groups of 3 to 4, open rapidly to form broad corollas full of bright copper-red petals, tending toward violet on the reverse. The slightly nodding habit of the flowers is typical of Tea roses; they are very pleasantly scented. Like the great majority of *R. odorata* (Tea rose) varieties, "Général Schablikine" does best in areas where the winters are not too harsh.
Use As an isolated specimen; also against a wall, where it will reach a height of 2 m. (6½ ft.).

48 PÂQUERETTE

Origin This rose was the first of a new class widely distributed under the incorrect name of Polyantha. The female parent was the climbing rose which, unknown to its discoverers, was named both *R. multiflora* and *R. polyantha*. For more than a century its branches, rooted from cuttings, have been used as rootstock. In around 1870 the grower and breeder J.B. Guillot of Lyons (the man who in 1867 had raised "La France," the first Hybrid Tea), using seeds taken from *R. multiflora* (a rambling shrub), probably pollinated by *R. chinensis pumila* (a dwarf shrub), obtained several low-growing, recurrent rose bushes, both characteristics derived from the male parent. From this group he chose one with small, double, clustered white flowers, calling it "Pâquerette." A second Polyantha, "Mignonette," was similar in habit but had deep red flowers; this was marketed in 1880 but, unlike its relative, does not seem to have been further cultivated.
Description The small green branches are almost thornless, the leaves are glossy, and the flowers appear early, continuing until autumn.
Use Good for edging a flower bed; does well, too, on the terrace or patio in a pot or basket.

49 ULRICH BRUNNER FILS

Synonym "Ulrich Brunner"
Origin Max Singer's *Dictionnaire des Roses* (1885), almost contemporary with "Ulrich Brunner Fils" (1881), vaguely describes it as "descended from Paul Neyron;" and recent descriptions have been equally ambiguous.
Description A sturdy rose with upright habit, growing almost 2 m. (6½ ft.) high; as a garden plant it can be kept shapely by pruning, which encourages thick growth. In spring the outer green branches can be bent almost horizontally and pegged down. Like the majority of Hybrid Perpetuals, it does best in clay soil; yet the 1910 Annual of the National Rose Society states: "it grows well everywhere like a weed." The double, globular flowers, fairly numerous in the first flowering period, grow from the tip of long stems; they tend to diminish during the summer but bloom once more in early autumn.
Use Notable for the number and beauty of the flowers, either in cut form or on the plant during the two principal flowering periods.

50 MME ISAAC PEREIRE

Origin A variety derived from *R. borboniana*, raised in France by M. Garçon (1881).
Description The 1980 Annual of the Royal National Rose Society reports on the symposium on Bourbons and Hybrid Perpetuals, in which leading British rose growers awarded overall pride of place, out of 42 candidates, to "Mme Isaac Pereire." Jack Harkness, whose book *Roses* (1978) is acknowledged to be the best on the subject, parts company with this opinion, describing the rose (here in conjunction with "Mme Ernst Calvat," a light pink sport of "Mme Isaac") as follows: "Their long branches are clad with dull foliage, nasty little thorns and mildew. Their flowers, revolting in color, frequently ameliorate that sin by failing to open at all ... The experts propose they should be grown as climbers; and for a wall facing a neighbor one wishes to annoy, they are ideal subjects." The contributors to the symposium praised its very agreeable, voluptuous pink flowers, particularly marvelous in autumn, and declared that for its perfume alone—stronger than that of almost any other rose—it deserved a place in the garden. Jack Harkness fails to understand the reason for the general applause. "Like Johnny the soldier," he writes, "I am at a loss to understand why the rest of the platoon persists in marching out of step."
Use A sturdy shrub which, with ideal soil conditions and an adequate support, becomes a climber.

51 CÉCILE BRUNNER

Synonyms "Mlle Cécile Brunner," "Sweetheart Rose," "Mignon"

Origin It was raised by Antoine Ducher's widow in 1881, the year her daughter Marie married Joseph Pernet, the grower who had given new colors to rose petals. Traditionally, the parents of this rose have been given as an unidentified Polyantha variety and the Tea rose "Mme de Tartas." However, the well-distanced small leaves suggest that the partner of the Tea rose was a hybrid of *R. chinensis*, and this is its present, although by no means agreed, classification.

Description There are three forms (dwarf, shrub and climbing) of "Cécile Brunner." The climbing form is dealt with elsewhere in this book; here we are concerned with the original dwarf form and the shrub which is its sport. In both types the pale pink buds have the small, neat shape required by florists, and a very pleasing perfume. The dwarf form flowers about ten days earlier than the other; both, but especially the shrub (known as "Spray Cécile Brunner"), are very free-flowering. The branches are almost without thorns and the buds are so sparse as to furnish little material for propagation; nevertheless the shrub form is easily multiplied by cuttings, the other a little less so.

Use The dwarf form is attractive in tight groups and in containers; the shrub can be grown on its own and in larger containers. They are unrivaled as cut flowers in bud.

52 POMPON DE BOURGOGNE

Synonym "Pompon de Mai"

Origin Classified among the Centifolia Pompons; at the beginning of the present century there were 110 varieties in this category. The origin of "Pompon de Bourgogne" is uncertain. There is a detailed description of the plant in Max Singer's *Dictionnaire des Roses* (1885), from which it appears that in spite of the single early flowering period, the rose was at that time widely known and appreciated.

Description A thick bush of 50–60 cm. (20–24 in.), with thin branches that bend when covered with small perfumed flowers; the petals are deep pink in the middle, larger and paler on the outside. The thorns are thin and numerous; the leaves are light green with three, often five, rarely seven leaflets. After flowering, old wood should be pruned at the base, as well as any branches which are making the adult plant too thick.

Use In groups of the same species. Individual specimens also show up well, given plenty of surrounding space.

53 MRS JOHN LAING

Origin A Hybrid Perpetual raised in 1887 by Henry Bennett, an English cattle breeder who some years previously had turned his hand to breeding roses, applying to them the same genetic principles as for animals.

Description It is worth recalling the favorable comments of the members chosen by a committee of the National Rose Society in 1910 to pass judgment on the garden roses of that time. Similar views were expressed by a group of experts assembled for the same purpose by the society some 70 years later, who described it as sturdy and vigorous, with an upright habit, doing well everywhere, but preferably in cool soil. It was voted the most floriferous and recurrent variety in its class. The flowers, at the tip of long stems, are of exhibition quality with double corollas, 10 cm. (4 in.) and more in width, highly fragrant, rose-pink with a touch of lilac.

Use Preferably for cut flowers. Watch out for mildew, even in late summer, and treat immediately.

---

54 MME CAROLINE TESTOUT

Origin Derived from a cross between "Mme de Tartas" (Tea) and "Lady Mary Fitzwilliam" (Hybrid Tea), and therefore included in the latter category. It was raised by Joseph Pernet-Ducher of Lyons. In real life Mme Caroline Testout was a celebrated dressmaker with a large and important clientele. In 1890, to coincide with the opening of the London branch of her fashion showrooms, she bought from the already famous grower an unnamed rose and all residual rights, mainly to call it "Mme Caroline Testout" and to use it as an advertisement for her name and her business throughout the world. This shrewd step exceeded all expectations because of the extraordinary success that this variety continued to enjoy for many decades; even today, almost a century later, it can hold pride of place in gardens alongside more recent introductions.

Description A vigorous, well-branched, floriferous bush; the many large petals are bright pink and slightly fragrant. In 1901 the grower Chauvry of Bordeaux marketed a climbing sport which is equally vigorous, free-flowering and recurrent and is the form usually grown today.

Use It is advisable to plant in groups of at least five bushes.

55 BLANC DOUBLE DE COUBERT

Origin *R. rugosa* x "Sombreuil" (Tea), raised in 1892 by the grower and breeder Cochet-Cochet, who was born and worked in the village of Coubert in the department of Seine et Marne. Some authors question whether the variety was the result of a planned cross, claiming it to have been a chance seedling of *R. rugosa alba.*

Description A vigorous shrub, slow-growing for the first two to three years; when adult it exceeds 2 m. (5–6 ft.) in height and will grow almost as wide unless kept in check by pruning. Like the great majority of Rugosa varieties, it is not subject to insect parasites, mildew or black spot. It does well even in semi-sandy soils, and—a rare gift—its large white semi-double flowers give off their fresh scent even at night. The characteristic Rugosa foliage is not as dense as in other varieties of the same species.

Use For hedging or in small, tight groups.

---

56 BARON GIROD DE L'AIN

Origin A sport from the Hybrid Perpetual "Eugène Fürst," which has red petals (lighter on the reverse), without the white edge that characterizes those of "Baron Girod de l'Ain." It has been marketed since 1897.

Description The bush is covered with large rippled leaves and the branches have sharp thorns. The main attraction is the globular, double, scented flowers, dark crimson with a thin white edge. This rare feature is also present in the flowers of "Roger Lambelin," another Hybrid Perpetual sport.

Use Apart from the white border to the petal, the rose is interesting for its globular corolla, its fragrance and its value as a cut flower.

57 SOLEIL D'OR

Origin Joseph Pernet-Ducher, creator of "Soleil d'Or," identified this variety as the second-generation offspring of a cross between his hybrid of *R. foetida persiana* (nonrecurrent) and "Antoine Ducher" (Hybrid Perpetual). It has been established, in fact, that when the characteristic of recurrence is present in only one of the parents, it will not appear in the first generation but in the second. On this point see the introduction, under the heading "Yellow petals for garden roses."

Description This was the first of the Pernetiana roses; before this, with the exception of a few pale creamy yellow Tea roses (and some of the Noisettes which were descended from them), yellow-petaled roses were unknown in garden displays. In spite of the suggestive name, "Soleil d'Or" can be compared neither with the sun nor with gold, although such comparisons could be made for its descendant, "Rayon d'Or" (1910). The foliage is subject to black spot.

Use Collector's rose.

58 FRAU KARL DRUSCHKI

Synonyms "Reine des Neiges," "Snow Queen," "White American Beauty"

Origin It was raised in 1901 by the German breeder Peter Lambert, who introduced his novelty in a competition for the best new German rose worthy to be named "Otto von Bismarck." Although the judges voted unanimously in favor of Lambert's rose, it was subsequently decided that its pure white petals were unsuitable to represent the Iron Chancellor, so it was rejected.

Description Certain of its antecedents suggested that it rightly belonged to the group of Hybrid Teas, and the pattern of the flower seems to confirm this; but the foliage, the vigorous growth, the habit and the two well-separated flowering periods are typical of the Hybrid Perpetuals.

Use Peg the longer branches almost horizontally. If the upright habit is preferred, the plant will benefit from the support of a medium-sized stake. Pruning should be kept to a minimum.

59 ROSERAIE DE L'HAŸ

Origin Introduced in France by Cochet-Cochet. There is dis-
agreement as to whether it is a sport of *R. rugosa rubra*, as
officially claimed. The variety was marketed in 1900. Jack
Harkness is of the opinion that it is probably a hybrid of *R.
rugosa rubra*, and warns against confusing it with the similarly
named "Rose à Parfum de l'Haÿ," which is less lovely and less
fragrant. "It would be a pity," he writes, "to buy it in error."
Description A vigorous large shrub with balanced growth, up to
2 m. (6 ft.). Tough, glossy leaves, disease-resistant, with the
typical crinkling of descendants of *R. rugosa*; the strongly
scented flowers are an interesting deep crimson, tending to
purple. The historic rose garden of Haÿ les Roses, after which
this variety is named, was created by Jules Gravereaux, who did
so much to improve and popularize roses in the nineteenth
century.
Use Free hedge; individual specimen.

60 VARIEGATA DI BOLOGNA

Origin A Bourbon or possibly Gallica variety, raised by Mas-
similiano Lodi for the Bonfiglioli nurseries of Bologna; marketed
in 1909.
Description A large, vigorous shrub with nondescript foliage,
flowers separate or in groups, globular perfumed, double, white
with reddish-violet stripes. The rose has a strong tendency to
produce a sport with uniformly red flowers. The first flowering is
very abundant and highly decorative, but recurrence is not
continuous. The characteristic petal stripes are attributed to
"Pride of Reigate," the presumed ancestor of "Variegata di
Bologna."
Use The generous growth of the shrub suggests single specimens, or eventually groups with other variegated roses.

61 FÉLICITÉ ET PERPÉTUE

Origin A hybrid of *R. sempervirens* raised in 1827 by A. Jacques, gardener to Louis Philippe, when Duc d'Orléans, at the latter's castle at Neuilly. The names are those of Jacques's daughters, themselves named after two girl martyrs, and the rose appears as such in the supplement to the *Calalogue des Roses cultivées chez Prévost Fils*, published in 1830. It is listed in the *Dictionnaire des Roses* (1885) as "Félicité Perpétuelle," implying recurrence which, however, is not characteristic. Together with "Adélaide d'Orléans," likewise a hybrid of *R. sempervirens*, it is among the very finest ramblers raised in Europe.

Description It flowers late, producing enormous numbers of white, double, flat, scented flowers opening from pink buds. Despite its Mediterranean ancestry (*R. sempervirens*), it also does well in zones that experience harsh winters. Only the lightest pruning is necessary, eliminating old and dead wood completely.

Use For covering walls or old trees, even in shady spots.

△ *Plates 61–75 represent climbing roses up to 1910.*

---

62 POMPON DE PARIS

Synonym "Climbing Rouletii"

Origin A climbing sport (*c.* 1830) from the original dwarf bush form, which is rarely grown nowadays; many growers consider it synonymous with *R. rouletii*, which is the name used in the United States and other countries (Penney and Krüssmann).

Description The climbing form exhibits numerous, thin and much-branched shoots which can cover a trellis of 2 sq. m. (20 sq. ft.); the small pointed leaves reveal its close relationship to *R. chinensis minima* and to *R. rouletii*. In spring, very early, it is covered in elegant little buds which open into small, flat, semi-double pink flowers; over the following months more flowers appear sporadically. Thrives on its own roots. This description of "Climbing Pompon de Paris" is based on observation of a specimen from the historic garden of Haÿ les Roses, cultivated for fifteen years in the author's garden.

Use For covering walls, fences and trellises.

63 LAURE DAVOUST

Origin A rambling rose bred in 1834 by M. Laffay at Meudon, outside Paris, where he raised 388 varieties. The antecedents are tentatively named as a variety of *R. sempervirens* or of *R. multiflora*.

Description Anyone seeing this variety for the first time in full flower must be charmed by the abundant, healthy clusters of double flowers in various shades of pink. Hard frosts may possibly impede its vigorous growth. G.S. Thomas states that the shoots grow to less than 2 m. (6½ ft.), but at Haÿ les Roses—and according to other authors—adult specimens will exceed 5 m. (16 ft.) in length.

Use Walls, fences and trellises.

64 GLOIRE DE DIJON

Origin A variety raised by Jacotot of Dijon (France) in 1853 from a cross of a Bourbon variety ("Souvenir de la Malmaison") with an unidentified Tea rose; so although classified among the climbing forms of what were once the Noisettes, it also shows typical characteristics of the Teas.

Description Vigorous but untidy growth habit; flowers are early, double, scented, buff-yellow with apricot tints; slightly recurrent. It is regarded as the most interesting of the climbing roses before the advent of modern varieties. There are signs—though not general—of an organic decline which has not been precisely diagnosed; a similar phenomenon has been encountered in some areas in the case of the related climbing variety "Maréchal Niel;" some attribute it to continuous propagation (grafting, cutting, layering), others to low temperatures.

Use Makes a happy contrast with a brick wall or a similarly colored background.

65 MARÉCHAL NIEL

Origin A climbing variety raised by Henri Pradel at Montauban (France) in 1864. It is thought to be the progeny of "Chromatella" (climbing Noisette), in its turn a seedling of a Noisette variety x Tea rose. The variety is named after Adolphe Niel, marshal of France, who distinguished himself in Algeria and the Crimea.

Description To get some idea of the esteem in which this variety was held, it is sufficient to recall that Pradel would not accept orders for "Maréchal Niel" alone; each order had to be accompanied by one for a dozen other higher-priced roses (cf. Royal National Rose Society Annual, 1931). In its time it was unequaled for vigor, foliage, flower color (the loveliest yellow anywhere) and perfume; it was just as highly valued in areas where, because winter temperatures fell below zero, the rose had to be grown in an unheated greenhouse. Today, in some places, it shows signs of decline.

Use Covering walls, fences or trellises in warm climates.

66 ZÉPHIRINE DROUHIN

Origin Bizot, France, 1868. The parents are not known but it certainly belongs to the Bourbons, being subsequently absorbed into the class of Hybrid Teas.

Description A climber of moderate growth with young branches which can be trained either almost horizontally or as a cover for tripods or pillars. It is advisable to give it a well-aired position, to prevent attacks of mildew. However, it is not harmed by industrial pollution, nor by alkaline soil up to pH=7.5. The almost complete absence of thorns has caused it to be known as the "thornless rose." The double flowers, cerise-pink and highly fragrant, appear very early and continue at intervals until the first frosts.

Use Trellises, fences, informal hedges, pillars.

67 MME ALFRED CARRIÈRE

Origin A climbing rose raised in 1879 by Joseph Schwartz of Lyons; during his lifetime Schwartz introduced 63 of his own varieties, and a further 57 were marketed by his widow. There is no information about its ancestors, but it exhibits characteristics midway between a Noisette and a Hybrid Tea.

Description When fully mature the branches can reach a height of more than 6 m. (20 ft.), retaining their green color for a long time. The very big double flowers, highly perfumed, lose within a few hours of opening the pale pink flush that initially suffuses the white of the petals. Unlike other old climbing roses, it shows no signs of deterioration.

Use Against a wall or trellis, or covering a pergola. Does not mind a partially shaded position.

68 CL. CÉCILE BRUNNER

Origin The climbing sport from the shrub was discovered in 1894 in California.

Description Graham Thomas, official biographer of old roses, states that nobody can claim to know "the rose" without having admired at least 14 varieties; and his list is topped by "Cécile Brunner," which elsewhere he describes as "unique." This judgment obviously applies equally to the climbing sport, because the flowers and leaves of the low shrub, bush and climbing forms are almost identical. The American Rose Society list of recommended varieties for 1986 places it among the class of "excellent" roses. In spite of certain doubts raised in other quarters, it bears an abundance of blooms after the first flowering period for as long as there are no night frosts to harm them. Pruning should be confined to removing weak and tangled branches, allowing the plant to occupy as much space as it needs; height can be kept in check by arranging the branches in a fan.

Use Large trellises or walls. Flowers for cutting.

69 ALBÉRIC BARBIER

Origin Raised from *R. wichuraiana* (white) x "Shirley Hibberd" (yellow Tea) by Barbier of Orléans, marketed in 1902. The Asiatic species *R. wichuraiana* and *R. luciae* are practically identical, but it must be remembered that some botanists suggest that one could be a variety of the other. In particular, during breeding experiments the species with the characteristics of *R. luciae* was used to raise—among others—both "Albéric Barbier" and another important climbing rose, "Alexandre Girault," (see entry 73).

Description A very vigorous rambler, up to 6–7 m. (20–23 ft.) high, with long, fairly flexible branches and shiny, dark green, persistent foliage. The small, well-shaped creamy buds open into medium-sized double, perfumed flowers with somewhat formless petals, white with an initial touch of yellow. It is slightly recurrent.

Use Large walls and pergolas.

70 DOROTHY PERKINS

Origin *R. wichuraiana* x "Mme Gabriel Luizet" (Hybrid Perpetual). The cross was made by E. Alwin Miller of the firm of Jackson & Perkins, Newark, New York; the variety was marketed in 1901. Dorothy Perkins was head of the household, mother of the founder of the above firm of growers.

Description This is a typical rambler, with long shoots that—especially when young—lend themselves easily to covering tripods and pergolas or to trailing from above. The dense foliage is glossy, but subject to attacks of mildew unless preventive treatment is applied and a well-aired site provided. The pink flowers, late-blooming and scentless, last for six or seven weeks; only in warm zones may there be sporadic flowering in the autumn, in which case it is as well to remove tangled shoots as soon as the first flowering is over. "Excelsa," a related variety with bright pink flowers, is known as the "Red Dorothy Perkins."

Use Fences, trellises and pergolas in airy positions. Weeping standards can be grafted on stems of about 2 m. (6½ ft.).

71 AMERICAN PILLAR

Origin The outcome of the cross *R. wichuraiana* x *R. setigera* was subsequently crossed with a red-flowered Hybrid Perpetual. This double procedure was concluded in 1902. The Asiatic *R. wichuraiana* was the parent of other rambling roses; *R. setigera* is an American species, also with one late seasonal flowering, and has affinities with the European *R. moschata*.

Description A rambler with flexible shoots 6–7 m. (20–23 ft.) long, and an abundance of glossy, bright green leaves. The flowers, with five petals, bright pink with a central white eye, are unscented and borne profusely in tight clusters. The single late flowering period lasts about one month. The rose is prone to attacks of mildew; it is advisable to thin out adult specimens, removing old wood as soon as flowering is over.

Use Pergolas, well-aired trellises, weeping standards.

72 BELLE PORTUGAISE

Synonym "Belle of Portugal"

Origin Raised by Henri Cayeux in the Lisbon Botanical Garden; the female parent was certainly *R. gigantea*, the date probably 1903.

Description The appearance of this rose and its vulnerability to low temperatures classify the variety as a hybrid of *R. gigantea*, more akin to the Tea roses. In warm climates and in protected positions elsewhere, its long shoots are covered very early in the season with strongly scented pale pink flowers which hang their heads in the typical manner of many Teas. Flowering is abundant, but limited to spring.

Use Big walls and fences, which are often entirely covered with shoots. Thrives best in Mediterranean and other warm climatic zones.

73 ALEXANDRE GIRAULT

Origin *R. wichuraiana* x "Papa Gontier" (Tea), raised by the firm of Barbier in Orléans; marketed since 1909.

Description The roses raised by Barbier are distinguished from others of the same origin produced in the United States particularly by virtue of the large semi-double flowers along the length of firm branches covered with glossy foliage, which contrasts effectively with the subsequent blooms. There is reason to believe, therefore, that the female parent was in some cases *R. wichuraiana*, in others the separate species *R. luciae*. It is exceptionally vigorous, and the single long flowering period produces a remarkable number of strawberry-red flowers with darker tints and a broad yellow patch at the base. (For the traditional use of "Alexandre Girault" in the historic rose garden of Haÿ les Roses, see also the spectacular double-spread photograph on pp. 70–1.) There is no need for drastic pruning of shoots when flowering is over, as recommended for the "Excelsa" variety (characterized by scentless inflorescences at the tip of the shoots), since "Alexandre Girault" exhibits scattered flowers along the entire length of the shoots.

Use Wide expanses, pergolas.

---

74 VEILCHENBLAU

Synonym "Violet Blue"

Origin "Crimson Rambler" (climbing hybrid of *R. multiflora*) x variety of *R. setigera*, raised by J.C. Schmidt of Erfurt, Germany, in 1909.

Description The almost thornless shoots, up to 4 m. (13 ft.) long, maintain their lovely green color for some time; the foliage is agreeably scented but even more so are the flowers, consisting of a dozen or so narrow petals with a white center and a color that has touches of violet, lilac and pink, seen to best effect in positions out of direct sunlight.

Use Fences, trellises, small walls.

75 LA FOLLETTE

Origin 1) A French term often used jokingly to describe a lively, somewhat giddy and unpredictable young woman. 2) According to the late Charlotte Testu, the variety was named after the U.S. senator and presidential candidate Robert M. La Follette. The rose was raised in Lord Brougham's garden at Cannes, in around 1910, by his head gardener Mr. Busby, who marketed it during the 1930s after his employer's death. Because of its great similarity to "Belle Portugaise," it is assumed to be a seedling of that variety, and like the latter it shows clear affinity with *R. gigantea*, one parent of the Tea rose. It is even thought that it may be the product of their crossing.

Description The extremely vigorous growth can cover a vast surface and provides an extraordinary profusion of early flowers over five to six weeks. The shapes of the buds and flowers are identical to those of the variety from which it presumably stemmed; the petals are a deeper pink and the perfume is equally pronounced.

Use A rose for a mild climate; elsewhere it needs a position well sheltered from cold winds or, even better, a cold greenhouse.

76 OPHELIA

Origin One of the most celebrated English rose nurseries of the nineteenth century was founded in 1860 by William Paul. In the autumn of 1909 the firm of William Paul & Son bought a parcel of "Antoine Rivoire" roses from Pernet-Ducher of Lyons; the following year they discovered one rose among the batch which was exceptional for its vigor, foliage, color and form of flower; its origin was a complete mystery.

Description This is a vigorous bush with long, stiff stems bearing pointed buds and exquisitely shaped flowers; for 50 years the latter have been a touchstone for judging other roses. The translucent petals are blush-pink, tinted pale yellow at the base, and are delicately yet strongly perfumed. It is safe to say that "Ophelia" and its descendants have influenced and set models for breeders who specialize in crossing varieties still inappropriately known as Hybrid Teas. In 1930 an excellent climbing sport was found. It is advisable to treat in spring against mildew, and also, as necessary, against thrips.

Use Bedding rose; flowers for cutting. The climbing form needs plenty of space.

◇ *Plates 76–173 represent garden roses from 1911 to the present day.*

77 MME EDOUARD HERRIOT

Synonym "Daily Mail Rose"
Origin "Mme Caroline Testout" x unknown variety probably a Pernetiana, already named Mme Edouard Herriot in France. The raiser, Joseph Pernet-Ducher, entered his variety for the International Exhibition held in London on May 22, 1912; the rose, with its petals of highly unusual color (a blend of coral-red, scarlet, pink and apricot), won the coveted gold cup awarded by the London *Daily Mail* for the best new variety, on condition that it should be called the "Daily Mail Rose." The double name was accepted as a compromise, though the original French name is generally used in the trade.
Description A none-too-vigorous shrub, of low growth, with large flat thorns. The climbing form, a sport raised by Ketten Frères, Luxembourg, 1921, proved even more successful; with its contained growth, it is useful for covering limited surfaces. The flowers, either single or several to the stem, open early, exhibiting the same unequaled color as the shrub form. Recurrence is not guaranteed but can be encouraged by a short period of summer drought followed by watering and quick-acting fertilizer application.
Use Bush form can be splendid for bedding. Climbing form needs only a low trellis, avoiding exposure to full sun.

78 PAUL'S SCARLET CLIMBER

Origin Raised in 1916 by William Paul & Son, England, using either *R. wichuraiana* or *R. luciae*.
Description Its principal attribute is the large number of scarlet flower clusters in the course of the single long flowering period. Growth is vigorous and the habit fairly upright; the branching shoots are firmer than the more flexible shoots of some other varieties (e.g. "Dorothy Perkins" and "Excelsa"). "Paul's Scarlet Climber" does not need annual rejuvenation by removing shoots at the base, as is recommended for varieties of the same origin with weaker branches; the same applies for "Albéric Barbier." For half a century "Paul's Scarlet Climber" has been the most popular garden climber (some say rambler), very sturdy and long-lived. In 1932 the variety "Blaze" was marketed, with the same attributes as "Paul's Scarlet Climber" but described as recurrent; it has not always been possible to confirm this.
Use Tripods, fences, pergolas and walls, though not in full sunlight.

79 MERMAID

Origin Hybrid of *R. bracteata* x (according to Jack Harkness) "Mme de Tartas;" introduced by William Paul of Waltham Cross, England, in 1918.
Description Despite all the years that have passed, this climber still merits pride of place for its vigorous growth, spreading branches, neat little glossy leaves (evergreen in suitable climates), large, single, scented yellow flowers, 12–13 cm. (about 15 in.) across, persistent amber stamens and—an incomparable attribute—for its continuity of flowering. The blooms appear rather late and retain their luminous color through to the autumn. "Mermaid" will even thrive against a wall without much sun. It needs no pruning to remove old wood or excess branches; it is not compatible with rootstock of *R. canina*; and it may be killed off by especially hard frosts and prolonged winter temperatures.
Use Large wall in temperate zones; in colder areas against a sunny wall.

80 MME BUTTERFLY

Origin A sport from the Hybrid Tea variety "Ophelia" (see entry 76), which appeared in 1918. The habit of "Ophelia" to produce sports was generally transmitted to its progeny. Ann P. White, in an article published in 1955 in the *Journal* of the Royal Horticultural Society, revealed that "Ophelia" had produced 36 sports and "Mme Butterfly" a further 13, all of them in their turn having originated others.
Description A bush of medium height—about 70 cm. (28 in.)—with upright branching habit, shoots from the base and sparse foliage. It has been widely cultivated under glass for its elegant, fragrant double flowers, pinkish-white with apricot tints, a color that distinguishes it from "Ophelia" although its corolla shape is the same. All these features make it slightly more popular than the original. It is very free-flowering in the garden as well, and here there is no need to disbud; this is necessary under glass, for the cut flower trade. In 1926 the English grower E.P. Smith marketed a climbing sport of "Mme Butterfly," characterized by excellent vigor and even lovelier flowers, blooming in late May and June with further sporadic appearances. Every other feature (small leaves, flower color, perfume) is like that of the bush.
Use Mainly cut flowers.

81 ETOILE DE HOLLANDE

Origin Raised by H.A. Verschuren, Holland, in 1919 from "General MacArthur" (an exceptionally floriferous Hybrid Tea) x "Hadley" (a well-shaped and scented Hybrid Tea).

Description A fairly free-flowering rose with scented, double flowers, the petals slightly muddled, ranging from scarlet to crimson with darker velvety flushes; very vigorous growth, almost thornless. For at least thirty years it has served as a touchstone for judging new red-flowered varieties and has been highly prized in gardens for its recurrence and the color and fragrance of the petals, which are, however, liable to "scorch" under hot sun. In 1931 the Dutch firm of Lenders marketed the climbing sport, which exhibits the same qualities of vigor, scent, color and recurrence. After a slow start it makes rapid progress over the years; specimens have been recorded with 135 flowering days in a single season.

Use Because the flowers develop very quickly and because the color is sensitive to hot sun, it does best in a slightly shaded position, where the corollas seem to grow even bigger. It is not always sturdy in areas with harsh winters.

82 VIOLETTE

Origin Raised in 1921 by the rose-growing firm of Turbat, still a leading name in the professional life of Orléans, one of France's most flower-bedecked cities. The parents of "Violette" are unknown but it is thought to be a seedling of "Crimson Rambler," a vigorous rambler possibly descended from *R. multiflora* with clusters of red flowers, fading to bluish. This was imported in 1893 from Japan, where it was called "Soukara-Ibara."

Description The shoots of this rambler are about 3 m. (10 ft.) long, fairly flexible, with small, flat, double flowers in clusters, maroon-red tending to purple, flowering once between the end of May and the end of June, depending on the local climate. Faintly scented. The purple-violet tone is strong but not uniform during the flowering period.

Use For trellises and arbors.

83 ALBERTINE

Origin *R. wichuraiana* x "Mrs Arthur Robert Waddell" (a Pernetiana dating from 1921). This is one of the rambling roses of the Barbier series (e.g. "Albéric Barbier" and "Alexandre Girault"), which, although descended from *R. wichuraiana* (or from *R. luciae*), do not have the flexible branches or the small, double, flattened flowers, blooming late in apical clusters, which characterize "Excelsa," "Dorothy Perkins" and similar varieties. It is now often classed as a climber.

Description If the growth period is long enough and the rose is supported by a trellis or fence, "Albertine" produces in late spring a wonderful display, the dense clusters of large, many-petaled flowers, light pink and fragrant, contrasting beautifully with the background of deep green foliage. Without support it grows into a shrub twice as wide as it is high, 2 ×4 m. (6½ ×13 ft.).

Use Tripods, trellises, pergolas; without support it needs plenty of space. It can also be used for hedging with other recurrent varieties in between.

84 ROSA ROULETII

Synonyms *R. chinensis minima*, "Pompon de Paris"

Origin and description The Swiss botanist Henri Correvon described his "discovery" in *Floraire*, an autobiographical volume published in Geneva in 1936. The incident occurred as follows: "In 1917 my friend Colonel Roulet saw on a windowsill in the village of Onnens (in the Swiss Jura, at a height of 1,176 m.) a small pot with a dwarf rose, free-flowering and remontant, which, according to its owners, had been grown by the same family for more than a century." The harsh climate and the restricted size of the pot, according to Correvon, had reduced its habit which, in any event, must certainly have been of small size right from the start. Roulet and Correvon, having taken a few cuttings and impressed by the ornamental qualities of the tiny rose, devoted themselves busily to its propagation, so much so that from 1920 onward *R. rouletii*, incorrectly raised to species rank by this name, gradually came to be marketed worldwide, and came to constitute the new class of Miniature roses. Correvon, basing his claim on the fact that the village where he had "discovered" the little rose was close to the home of the botanist A. Pyramus de Candolle (1778–1841), and that the latter had described in his *Prodomus* a *R. indica humilis* (today *R. chinensis minima*), deduced from this that it must have been the originator of the so-called *R. rouletii*.

Use Small pots, flower boxes, edges of flower bed.

85 LAWRENCE JOHNSTON

Synonym and origin The seedling that originated the variety illustrated here was bought directly (around 1923) from the breeder Joseph Pernet-Ducher by Lawrence Johnston, an enthusiastic and knowledgeable plant collector, owner of Hidcote Manor in Gloucestershire, whose delightul gardens he himself laid out at the beginning of the twentieth century. Major Johnston called his rose "Hidcote Yellow," and it belonged to him until 1947 when Graham Thomas, adviser to the gardens owned by the National Trust, obtained permission to introduce and market it under the name "Lawrence Johnston."

Description The shining golden-yellow of the paternal parent *R. foetida persiana* is reflected in the semi-double perfumed flowers which cover the long branches plentifully for a couple of months in early summer, strikingly contrasted with the glossy, bright green foliage.

Use To cover broad areas of wall or trellis.

86 ROSE MARIE VIAUD

Origin and description Raised from a seedling of "Veilchenblau" (1924), it is named after the daughter of one of the growers who introduced it (Viaud-Bruant). It is an improvement on the variety from which it stemmed, with a deeper purple color, double flowers and large, unscented clusters which bloom from late spring or early summer, depending on climate. The shoots grow to 4–5 m. (13–16 ft.) if trained along a wall and are covered with light green leaves, prominently veined. The stems are practically thornless; the flower stalks are very subject to mildew.

Use Train along a trellis or fence, to allow plenty of air. Alternatively, as a bush with the long branches initially erect, then trailing.

87 NEVADA

Origin "Nevada" was raised from a Hybrid Tea ("La Giralda") in 1925 by the Spanish grower Pedro Dot, who crossed the latter with *R. moyesii* (or, according to Jack Harkness, with *R. spinosissima hispida*) In later years the nonagenarian Pedro Dot (who died in 1976), the father of roses in Spain, seldom left his garden at San Feliu de Llobregat for fear that he might die far from his beloved roses. In around 1936, at more or less the same time as the Dutch grower Jan de Vink was marketing his Miniature variety "Peon," Pedro Dot was also busy raising this type of rose, which seemed to be becoming popular with the public. The Civil War, however, delayed introduction of the varieties successfully raised in Spain.

Description In spring the branches of "Nevada," over 2 m. (6½ ft.) high and just as wide, are crowded with masses of creamy white flowers. They are single (rarely with a few additional petals) and very large; are white in the first profuse spring–summer flowering period, but gradually exhibiting more pronounced touches of pink in later, more sparse appearances and in hot weather. There is a sport, "Marguerite Hilling," identical to the original plant except for the marbled pink of its petals.

Use Individual specimens with plenty of surrounding space. Informal hedge.

88 MME GRÉGOIRE STAECHELIN

Synonym "Spanish Beauty"

Origin The second important variety raised by Pedro Dot (1927), from "Frau Karl Druschki" x "Château de Clos Vougeot." Forty years later it was given the Royal Horticultural Society's Award of Merit. The American rose expert and author J. Horace McFarland wrote in 1936 that had it not been handicapped by its unpalatable name, "Mme Grégoire Staechelin" would have been without peer in the rose world. It won top prize for new roses in the 1927 International Trials at Bagatelle.

Description A vigorous climbing rose with luxuriant, glossy, dark green foliage; reliably sturdy except in sites subject to particularly severe winters. There is one abundant and early flowering period in spring; the flowers are very large, semi-double and perfumed; the petals, in various shades of pink, are deeper toned on the outside. It can be successfully propagated by cuttings or by layering. To stimulate the production of strong shoots, initially reduce their number.

Use For covering walls, fences, trellises and pergolas, even in partial shade.

89 MRS PIERRE S. DU PONT

Origin The outcome (1929) of a complex series of crossings between several Pernetiana varieties ("Rayon d'Or," "Souvenir de Claudius Pernet," "Constance"), possibly with the addition of "Ophelia," although authors state that parents are unknown; it did, however, arrive in England among a batch of roses from the originator of the Pernetianas, Joseph Pernet-Ducher. The raiser of "Mrs Pierre S. Du Pont" (probably originally "Mme Pierre S. Du Pont") was Charles Mallerin, the amateur rose grower and expert breeder who taught François Meilland, the latter subsequently repaying the debt by naming a fine rose after him.

Description This was the loveliest golden-yellow rose of its day; the color had never previously been achieved in a garden rose and was suitably recognized by the jury at the Bagatelle Rose Trials of 1919, who awarded the variety its gold medal. The climbing sport which appeared in Texas in 1933 was even more popular and is still esteemed today, occupying a prominent place in the fine rose garden of Madrid.

Use The climbing form, for covering fences and pergolas, merits special attention.

90 TALISMAN

Origin From "Ophelia" x "Souvenir de Claudius Pernet," raised by the Montgomery Company of Hadley, Massachusetts, in 1929. This variety inherited from the latter parent its colors (golden-yellow with flushes of scarlet) and from the former its perfume and its tendency to produce new varieties through sports.

Description Despite having not too many petals (about 25), "Talisman," during the 1930s, was cultivated in the greenhouse for winter flowers because of its predisposition to produce a large number of virtually uniform flowering stems; but it also found a ready response for outdoor garden use. It was even more popular in the form of a climbing sport with the same features as the bush (single-flowering stems, color and petal scent); this remained in American and European catalogs until the 1960s.

Use As a bush, in the flower bed or for cut flowers in a separate section of the garden; climbing form for espaliers and trellises.

91 PRESIDENT HERBERT HOOVER

Origin The mixture of colors displayed by the petals indicates the presence of Pernetiana roses, its parents being "Sensation" x "Souvenir de Claudius Pernet." This very important variety was raised in 1930 by L.B. Coddington of New Jersey and was introduced on the day Herbert Hoover became President of the United States.

Description The principal characteristics of this variety are its vigor and rather leggy habit—the angular branches tending to grow upward—its large buds with curved red edges, its long-stemmed flowers with scented pink, orange and yellow petals, and its free flowering and recurrence. From 1930 to 1950 it enjoyed tremendous popularity as a bedder and as a greenhouse variety for cut flowers. A year after its introduction a vigorous climbing form appeared. This likewise became extremely successful and still thrives strongly in many gardens.

Use In modern rose collections.

---

92 CONDESA DE SÀSTAGO

Origin A double hybridization carried out by Pedro Dot, starting with a red-flowered Polyantha ("Maréchal Foch") and one of the first Pernetianas ("Souvenir de Claudius Pernet"); the progeny was in turn crossed with "Margaret McGredy", an ancestor of "Peace." "Condesa de Sàstago" won the Gold Medal for new roses from abroad at the inaugural trials of the Premio Roma in 1933. The previous year it had taken the first Certificate of Merit at the Bagatelle trials.

Description This bicolored rose has large corollas of 50 or more scented petals, the upper side flame-red, the underside golden-yellow, seen to fine advantage against the lovely glossy foliage. It is strongly recurrent and not subject to disease. A climbing sport which appeared in the United States in 1936 was quickly forgotten.

Use The original rose was widely used for creating ample patches of color in the garden.

93 NEW DAWN

Origin A recurrent sport from nonrecurrent "Dr. W. Van Fleet," itself the result of a double hybridization (*R. wichuraiana* x "Safrano") x "Souvenir du Président Carnot"—i.e. (botanical species x Tea Rose) x Hybrid Tea. Its recurrence, not originally present in "Dr. W. Van Fleet," was discovered in a specimen growing in the rose gardens of Henry A. Dreer of Philadelphia; the sport was named "New Dawn," propagated and marketed in 1930 by the Somerset Rose Nurseries. In that same year the United States introduced legislation for the protection of new plants, and "New Dawn" held Patent No. 1 under the Plant Patents Act.

Description A climbing rose of vigorous growth with beautiful shiny leaves and flexible branches of moderate length during the first two to three years. The flowers, growing singly or in clusters, are pale pink, perfumed, semi-double; averagely large, they bloom in abundance early in the year, more sparingly afterwards until autumn.

Use A continuously expanding climber, suitable for pillars, for forming weeping standards, as isolated specimens and as free-standing hedges.

94 COMTESSE VANDAL

Origin Its ancestors include "Ophelia" and "Souvenir de Claudius Pernet," two varieties which generated a large number of other important roses. It was raised in 1931 in the greenhouses of M. Leenders & Co., nowadays Jan Leenders Export Nurseries.

Description "Comtesse Vandal" was one of the most successful varieties of the interwar period, and at the end of the 1950s it still held pride of place in many gardens. The shrub is amply provided with basal shoots and has large glossy leaves, liable to be sensitive to hard frosts and to mildew in poorly aired sites. Descriptions at the time of introduction defined the long bud shape as "perfect," and the slightly curved, perfumed petals as "a pale, warm salmon-pink, copper-pink on the reverse." The climbing form, discovered in the United States in 1936, has the same types of flowers and leaves; it was popular for a while in gardens.

Use For display or separately for cut flowers.

95 THE FAIRY

Origin The result of a cross between the dwarf Polyantha rose "Paul Crampel" and the rambler "Lady Gay," a hybrid of *R. wichuraiana*. It was marketed in 1932 by J.A. Bentall of Romford.

Description It has a spreading habit, growing to 60–90 cm. (24–36 in.), with dense, healthy foliage. The leaves are small, bright green and very shiny; the flowers scented, double, in flat rosettes, the thick clusters being very plentiful during the long flowering period from late spring to the end of summer. The pale pink of the petals may tend to fade in intense summer heat; all things considered, it can bear comparison with many more recent varieties.

Use For ground cover or as a sturdy shrub with the branches trailing freely.

96 WILHELM

Synonym "Skyrocket" (USA)

Origin From "Robin Hood" x "J.C. Thorton" (Kordes, 1934); because of its lineage it is regarded as a Hybrid Musk, the only one of the group with red flowers but almost without scent, which distinguishes it from the ancestral species.

Description It grows to about 2 m. (6 ft.) high and half as wide. It is evenly branched, almost thornless. During the first, very abundant flowering, the entire plant is covered with deep crimson semi-double flowers, which then diminish in number until the frosts arrive. It is a healthy shrub, sturdy and without special needs.

Use As a specimen, in groups or for hedging.

97 CRIMSON GLORY

Origin Dr. Alfred Thomas, the eminent Australian grower, described Wilhelm Kordes (1891–1976) as the greatest of all rose breeders. In the course of his assiduous experiments it was his ambition to obtain a "Mme Caroline Testout" with red petals, a goal in which he had always been encouraged by his father, the founder of the family business. After some 25 years of increasingly perfected rose breeding, Wilhelm achieved and perhaps surpassed this objective when he produced "Crimson Glory," the most beautiful and most fragrant red rose of its time; as was predictable, "Mme Caroline Testout" had been a determining presence in the family tree.

Description A bush of medium height with upright habit. The foliage is prone to mildew. The double flowers are beautifully shaped and have a strong scent; they are carried on a short stem and tend to take on a purplish tone in strong direct sunlight. The rose does not need hard pruning. The climbing sport (moderately recurrent) which was introduced in 1946 is considered superior for flower quality to the bush variety.

Use As a bedder, but not in full sun.

98 PEON

Synonym "Tom Thumb"

Origin The first Miniature rose in the official register (*Modern Roses*). Raised in 1935–6 by Jan De Vink of Boskoop, Holland, it was bred from *R. rouletii* x "Gloria Mundi" (Polyantha). The Conard-Pyle Co., anticipating keen public interest, introduced it to the United States and the original name was replaced by the more appropriate "Tom Thumb" to emphasize its dwarf characteristics.

Description A compact little shrub, growing in the open to a maximum height of about 20 cm. (8 in.), thornless, with small light green leaves; very floriferous, with semi-double flowers growing singly or in clusters, the petals pink with a white center, lacking perfume.

Use For pots and window-boxes; between paving stones and at the edges of a flower bed.

99 BALLERINA

Origin A chance seedling in the nursery of J.A. Bentall, introduced by him in 1937.

Description A dense low-growing shrub, best classed as a Polyantha. In the initial flowering period the small glossy leaves are almost completely covered by innumerable trusses of single, light pink flowers with a white eye; these recur in lesser quantities. The flowers are strongly resistant to rain, but faded blooms should be removed immediately, or they will remain shriveled on the plant for some time. In the same year (1937) the German breeder Peter Lambert introduced his variety "Mozart," virtually identical to "Ballerina" but with bigger and less glossy leaves and more deeply colored petal margins.

Use Single specimens, hedges, standards.

100 GUINÉE

Origin Charles Mallerin, that alchemist of interesting and unusual colors, bred this "blackest" of red roses in 1938 from "Souvenir de Claudius Denoyel" x "Ami Quinard." Both were Hybrid Teas, the former valued for its highly scented, beautifully shaped scarlet flowers, the latter—also raised by Mallerin in 1930—with the unique advantage of red petals darker in tone than any known hitherto.

Description From the start a vigorous climber with perfectly shaped, highly fragrant double flowers, blood-red with darker, velvety, almost black tints. For guaranteed recurrence it is best to delay the first flowering by removing the first buds as soon as they form. Attacks of mildew can be combated with one or two applications of a systemic fungicide at the same time as the plant is treated against aphids with liquid insecticide.

Use The very dark color of the flowers is shown to excellent effect against a white or light-colored wall or blue sky.

101 PILAR LANDECHO

Synonym "Marquesa de Urquijo."

Origin This variety, raised by Rosas Camprubi di Llobregat of Barcelona, was introduced in 1938. It was to have been dedicated to the Marquesa de Urquijo but this was not an opportune moment in Spain to pay specific homage to a member of the nobility; so it was deemed prudent to commemorate the lady by her maiden name of Pilar Landecho.

Description A healthy, vigorous bush with erect habit and single-flower stems. The flowers are well shaped, double, with broad perfumed petals in a delicate shade of yellow flushed orange on the outside. Apart from being used for display in the garden, it is widely grown for cut flowers both in the open and under glass. It received the Gold Medal at the 1938 Bagatelle trials. In 1954 the firm of Comes Folgado of Valencia marketed the climbing sport, probably too late to take advantage of the popularity enjoyed before the war by the bush form.

Use See the description.

---

102 GLORY OF ROME

Synonyms "Gloria di Roma," "Gloire de Rome."

Origin Domenico Aicardi, the most experienced Italian breeder, raised this variety in 1938 from "Dame Edith Helen" (a lovely florists' rose from the Irish breeder Alexander Dickson) x "Sensation" (a traditional American garden variety with scented scarlet flowers). By crossing "Dame Edith Helen" and "Julien Potin" and "Julien Potin" with "Sensation," Aicardi obtained "Eternal Youth" in 1939 and "Signora" in 1936. These and other varieties from Aicardi were the first roses exported elsewhere in Europe and to the United States. "Glory of Rome" could be used either as a greenhouse plant for florists or as a garden bedding variety, like the translucent "Eternal Youth." "Signora" made an excellent bedder and was also grown for cut flowers, but in the open.

Description A moderately vigorous rose with sturdy branches and dark green leaves prone to mildew; straight flower stems carrying single or a few blooms; free-flowering and slightly recurrent. The large, deep cherry-red flower on its long, stiff stalk was virtually perfect in form with some 50 consistent, well-shaped, scented petals.

Use For cut flowers and in flower beds.

103 FRÜHLINGSMORGEN

Origin A seedling from the cross of two Hybrid Tea varieties ("E.G. Hill" x "Catherine Kordes"), fertilized with pollen from *R. spinosissima altaica*. Thus two double-flowered, scented, deep red varieties produced a seedling which was in its turn crossed with a very vigorous species with single, pale creamy-white, nonrecurrent flowers (W. Kordes, 1941).

Description Large, early-blooming, single flowers, about 12 cm. (5 in.) across; scented, a delicate cherry-pink with a yellow center and a tuft of amber stamens and anthers. After the first flowering a few blooms appear at intervals in late summer. The rose is upright in habit, almost 1·5 m. (5 ft.) high and nearly 1·25 m. (4 ft.) wide; the grey-green foliage is healthy. It appears in the pedigree of Sam McGredy's "hand-painted roses."

Use For specimen planting (supported by central stake); hedges.

104 PEACE

Synonyms "Mme A. Meilland" (original name), "Gloria Dei" (Germany), "Gioia" (Italy)

Origin There are conflicting accounts of its parentage, complicated by the fact that propagating wood was despatched from France during World War II to certain European countries and overseas. It is certain, however, that in June 1935, at Tassin-les-Lyon, the young Francis Meilland embarked on a long series of crosses with pollen from a selected seedling and eventually produced his "rose of the century." The exceptional qualities of "Peace" were soon evident and in the summer of 1939, with war threatened, the firm began supplying its distributors abroad with propagating material.

Description Norman Young, in *The Complete Rosarian*, summed it up as follows: "Flowers, leaves and habit give the impression of a normal rose, but seen through the lens of a magnifying glass." "Peace" was the first variety to be awarded the title of "World's Favorite Rose" by the World Federation of Rose Societies. In 1950 a climbing form appeared in the United States, with the same characteristics as the bush; nevertheless, freedom of flowering and recurrence may vary considerably either because of climatic conditions or because of indiscriminate use of unselected stock for propagation.

Use In groups or in homogeneous beds; flowers can also be grown for cutting. Distance between plants about 1 m. (3 ft.).

Synonym "Direktor Benschop" (original name)

Origin Raised by Mathias Tantau in the early years of World War II, the rose was introduced in Europe and the United States in 1945. The maternal parent is "Dorothy Perkins," a nonrecurrent Wichuraiana, and the pollinator "Professor Gnau," a Large-Flowered variety raised by Tantau himself with a complex family tree that includes three Hybrid Perpetuals and a Tea rose.

Description Vigorous, sturdy climber, well branched and of moderate height. Persistent glossy foliage; scented white flowers, semi-double (from 3 to 10 on the same stem), fairly rounded, early-blooming, long-lasting in the only flowering season. Except for its more compact growth, it resembles "Albéric Barbier."

Use Pergolas, arches, trellises.

106 MICHÈLE MEILLAND

Origin Meilland, 1945. The parents have been given as "Joanna Hill" and "Peace," but it must be mentioned that the former—in turn the offspring of "Mme Butterfly"—is also one of the ancestors of "Peace." There are, in fact, few traces of the latter, whereas the influence of "Joanna Hill" and "Mme Butterfly" is evident. Michèle Meilland (now Mme Raymond Richardier) is the daughter of the late Francis, and sister to Alain who, with his mother, Louisette Meilland, now runs one of the most successful rose-growing firms in France.

Description A vigorous and free-flowering bush; the slender buds open into large scented petals of the most delicate pink, flushed here and there with hints of yellow and orange. "Michèle Meilland" was one of the earliest descendants of "Peace;" in June 1945 it received the Bagatelle Gold Medal. In 1951 it produced a climbing sport which duplicates the features of the bush form but has even more vigor.

Use Apart from the normal uses (the bush for bedding, the climber for pergolas), some specimens yield good cut flowers. It is advisable to carry out a couple of treatments in spring to counteract mildew.

107 FRENSHAM

Origin Albert Norman, who raised this variety, was by profession a diamond setter who indulged his rose-growing hobby at his home in Surrey; he became an expert breeder and was eventually President of the National Rose Society. In 1946 Jack Harkness introduced Norman's two new roses: "Frensham," a Floribunda, and "Ena Harkness," a Hybrid Tea. Both became enormously successful, having been awarded the NRS Gold Medal in 1943 and 1945 respectively; and both produced climbing forms.

Description "Frensham" was for many years unrivaled for its deep crimson semi-double flowers, borne from spring to autumn, for its vigorous growth, for the manner in which its petals dropped of their own accord after fading, for its glossy foliage, etc. In 1955 it received the ARS Gold Certificate, awarded to the variety displaying the best performance for five consecutive years. Then it declined, as it unexpectedly became the particular victim of an unknown, virulent strain of mildew, to which the answer only now appears to have been found.

Use Patches of color in flower beds, standards, hedges.

---

108 CHARLES MALLERIN

Origin ("Glory of Rome" (Aicardi, 1938) x "Congo") x "Tassin" (Meilland, 1942). The first assured its double use as a cut flower and a bedder, the last contributed the penetrating perfume, the almost black color and the sparsely branching habit. The retired railwayman Charles Mallerin, who produced such unusual roses, had persuaded the young Francis Meilland to take up serious rose breeding; and the pupil gratefully dedicated his first rose to his mentor. At Lyons in 1947, the year it was introduced, it won the title of the "loveliest rose in France."

Description Both the bud and the half-opened flower are near-perfect in shape; then, as it opens completely, the corolla reveals its 35 large, richly scented petals, their velvety scarlet tinged almost black. Ideally it could yield more flowers, be more strongly recurrent and bear more basal shoots.

Use Although some later varieties flower more freely, "Charles Mallerin" is still a useful garden rose for cutting.

109 VIRGO

Synonym "Virgo Liberationem"
Origin "Blanche Mallerin" x "Neige Parfum" (Charles Mallerin, 1947). Mention has already been made of Charles Mallerin, the amateur rose grower who became famous as a breeder of unusual varieties. Just before World War II Mallerin bet some of his friends that he would produce, within five years, a Hybrid Tea with both white and scented flowers, something hitherto believed unattainable. In 1939, after exactly five years, Mallerin introduced "Neige Parfum," the male parent of "Virgo;" it was the first white, perfumed modern garden rose. Years later, without the incentive of a bet, Mallerin set about producing another variety with white flowers suitable for cutting; the result was "Virgo."
Description Forty years after its appearance it is possible to criticize some aspects of this variety (its limited yield of cut flowers, the faint flush of another color in the initial phases and the non-too-vigorous growth), but overall judgments must be positive. Its pollen has been used to create another recent, much-admired variety, "Iceberg."
Use Among the white specimens of any rose collection.

---

110 FASHION

Origin Raised in 1949 by Eugene S. Boerner (breeder of the American firm Jackson & Perkins Co.) from "Pinocchio" (="Rosenmärchen") x "Crimson Glory."
Description "Fashion" inherited the pelargonin gene, producing the striking orange color typical of certain geraniums; the tone had appeared in rose petals some 20 years before, but never so brilliantly. The end result was a delightful coral to salmon-pink color which, with the elegant flower shape and the marked floriferous qualities of the plant, aroused a great deal of interest and paved the way for various awards in Europe and the United States. After a couple of years the same firm introduced "Vogue," said to have sprung from a seed (achene) present in the same "fruit" containing the seed of "Fashion;" its flowers were cherry to coral-red.
Use In a group all of the same variety. Some spraying may be needed against mildew and later against rust (at least where the latter is a habitual nuisance).

111 MASQUERADE

Origin Raised in 1949 by Eugene S. Boerner, often described as the "father of Floribunda roses." Two botanical species figure in "Masquerade's" family tree: *R. foetida bicolor*, with bicolored red and yellow flowers; and *R. foetida persiana*, with yellow flowers.

Description A shrub with strong basal shoots, vigorous but of low to medium size, 50 cm. (20 in.); tough, glossy foliage. The clusters of semi-double flat flowers, 5 cm. (2 in.) across, turn from bright yellow to orange-pink and, just before fading, to dark red. It is very free-flowering and recurrent. A climbing form which appeared in 1958 did not have the success of the original rose, apparently because of its lack of vigor and almost nonexistent recurrence.

Use Planted in mass, quite close together, 40–50 cm. (16–20 in.) apart; also as a standard.

112 SUTTER'S GOLD

Origin "Charlotte Armstrong," one of the great successes of the Armstrong Nurseries in California (1940), and "Signora" ("Piero Puricelli"), the pre-war Italian bestseller, produced a truly worthy descendant in "Sutter's Gold." The name was chosen to commemorate the centenary (1840–1940) of the discovery of gold in Sutter's Creek, California.

Description Somewhat slow to establish itself, the bush can easily reach 1 m. (3 ft.) in height, with long, almost thornless branches covered with sparse, very glossy deep green leaves. The highly scented flowers are at their best in the early phase when an attractive red flush suffuses the basic golden-yellow, the red tone tending to predominate as the blooms quickly open. The rose does best in a temperate-cool climate.

Use For bedding.

113 CHRYSLER IMPERIAL

Origin From "Charlotte Armstrong" x "Mirandy" (both red roses, the latter variety being an offspring of the former). Raised by Dr W.E. Lammerts of California (1952), this rose undoubtedly has more merits and fewer defects than some critics care to admit. On its appearance it was included in the All-America Rose Selection, and 35 years later it still received 8.2 points out of 10 in the official listing of the American Rose Society. It is comparable to the English variety "Josephine Bruce" in its color, fragrance and tendency to mildew. In 1957 the rose was awarded the ARS Gold Certificate.

Description A moderately vigorous bush with erect, compact habit, so that it can be grown in quite small gardens. The leaves are large, mat dark green. The highly perfumed flowers are deep red and tend to go blue as they fade. In wet areas they may be attacked by mildew and rust.

Use Perfume, color and shape make it ideal for cutting.

---

114 TIFFANY

Origin In 1954 the Californian grower Robert V. Lindquist raised this variety from "Charlotte Armstrong" (red flowers) x "Girona" (bicolored, highly scented red and yellow flowers); it inherited the balanced growth and long stems of the former and the glowing petal color of the latter.

Description Vigorous rose which can grow more than 1 m. (3 ft.) high, with upright habit and all the attributes of an ideal variety. The glowing, deeply fragrant petals exhibit changing tones of pink, yellow and salmon; the slender buds open into beautifully formed flowers present from spring to autumn; and the long stems are perfect for cutting. It can withstand some periods of drought in the garden, but not rain, which damages the blooms. It was one of the three roses chosen in 1955 by the All-America Rose Selection.

Use For bedding and for cut flowers.

115 SPARRIESHOOP

Origin Sparrieshoop is the site of the extensive nurseries of Kordes, the rose growers, in Schleswig-Holstein, Federal Republic of Germany. This shrub shows the value of resorting to botanical species in hybridization, even if they seem to point in unknown directions. The pollen came from "Magnifica," a second-generation descendant of *R. eglanteria*, and was used to fertilize a seedling from "Baby Château" x "Else Poulsen," two Cluster-Flowered roses. The very sturdy, vigorous rose derived from this cross was introduced by Wilhelm Kordes in 1953.

Description A shrub with fairly upright habit, growing more than 2 m. (6½ ft.) high; the branches and young leaves are mahogany-red, the adult leaves dark green, tough and shiny. The single six-petaled flowers are large and are produced in great numbers during the first early flowering period, then more sparsely at intervals; they are bright pink and pleasantly scented, with prominent yellow stamens. The variety can withstand extremes of hot and cold.

Use Individual specimens (supported if necessary by tripods); hedges and up walls.

---

116 QUEEN ELIZABETH

Origin In 1954 Dr. W.E. Lammerts raised this variety for Germain's Nursery of Los Angeles from "Charlotte Armstrong" x "Floradora;") its family tree incorporated 18 crosses involving such famous names as "Soleil d'Or," "Ophelia," "Mme Caroline Testout" and "Crimson Glory." "Queen Elizabeth," exceptionally vigorous and upright, free-flowering and recurrent, was the first example of what the Americans call Grandifloras (a term not much used in Europe), characterized by clusters of large, well-formed flowers, like large Floribundas.

Description Given the right soil and climate, it will grow to 2.5 m. (8 ft.), and often much more. The clear pink flowers, with some 35 petals, are cup-shaped, almost scentless, and borne on virtually thornless long stems, sometimes singly but much more frequently in clusters. The dark green foliage is healthy. In 1979, at the meeting of the World Federation of Rose Societies in Pretoria, South Africa, it was given the title of "World's Favorite Rose." The majority of constituent societies voted for "Queen Elizabeth," which was the second rose to receive such recognition, the first having been "Peace" in 1976. The ARS also awarded the variety its Gold Certificate in 1960.

Use Individual specimens, groups, hedges; also good for cutting.

117 GOLDEN WINGS

Origin This is a hybrid from two crosses: "Sœur Thérèse" (large yellow rose with red borders) x (*R. spinosissima altaica* x "Ormiston Roy," itself a hybrid of *R. spinosissima*). The second cross, in 1956, was therefore between nonrecurrent roses, and the pronounced recurrence of "Golden Wings" stems from "Sœur Thérèse" and its antecedents. It was raised by the American grower Roy Shepherd, collector of old roses and author of *History of the Rose.*

Description A vigorous shrub, about 2 m. (6½ ft.) high and wide; few thorns, abundant mat foliage. Its chief glory is the fragrant, cream-yellow, large semi-double flowers, about 12 cm. (5 in.) across, which bloom from late spring to late autumn; in shape and color they resemble the flowers of "Mermaid." In the symposium on the best shrub roses, organized in 1972 by the Royal National Rose Society, "Golden Wings" gained first place, receiving the votes of five of the six judges.

Use Individual specimens; hedges.

118 COCKTAIL

Origin Raised by Francis Meilland in 1954 from crosses involving three varieties: "Independence" (Floribunda), "Orange Triumph" (Polyantha which subsequently produced a climbing sport) and "Phyllis Bide" (rambler). Meilland—despite the fact that this rose is still found in gardens—recently reused the name "Cocktail" for a lovely yellow florists' rose. This expedient of making repeated use of a striking name is due to the shortage of names in general and the high cost of patents.

Description Various explanations have been given of the origin of the term "cocktail," including romantic tales of girls or princesses pouring liquors of different colors (e.g. red, yellow and white) into the same glass and, more literally, the colored feathers of a cock's tail. In any event, this rose produces a similar mixed effect, thanks to its single cup-shaped flowers with a broad red border and a creamy yellow center which, after a couple of days, is merged into the red. It is also notable for its long flexible branches, its abundance of flowers and its recurrence.

Use Climber or standard with drooping branches; can be grown as a shrub.

119 ROSE GAUJARD

Origin Jean Gaujard, inheritor of the tradition and business of the rose-growing firm of Pernet-Ducher, in producing this variety in 1957 followed the broad principles of his predecessors, choosing to cross "Peace" with a seedling of "Opera," both of which had, among their known ancestors, *R. foetida persiana* and *R. foetida bicolor*.

Description A bush which probably owes its vigorous growth to "Peace," as well as its balanced branching habit and its large glossy leaves; the warm bicolored petals indicate its descent from "Opera." The white ground of the corollas is flushed with carmine, which suffuses the broad borders, and the reverse is silver-white. The abundant recurrence, especially in autumn, the length of time the flowers remain on the plant and their resistance to atmospheric pollution all make "Rose Gaujard" an excellent garden variety. In addition the numerous single-stemmed flowers are slightly fragrant, and the plant itself is healthy and vigorous, easy to grow.

Use In the flower bed, planted at intervals of 60–70 cm. (24–28 in.); also good for cutting.

---

120 SARABANDE

Origin Francis Meilland raised "Sarabande" in 1957 from two of his previous Cluster-Flowered varieties, "Cocorico" x "Moulin Rouge."

Description A low bush with spreading habit, large leaves and big flowers with six to nine petals; the very bright color varies with the intensity of the sun, the soil and the season, ranging from geranium-red through orange to scarlet, with contrasting yellow stamens. It is one of the few roses with very few petals to have collected gold medals at international trials (Baden Baden, Geneva, Portland, Rome) and was one of three winners of the All-America Rose Selection in 1960. It is very free-flowering and recurrent, but with no scent.

Use Patches of color in the flower bed.

121 CENTENAIRE DE LOURDES

Synonym "Mrs Jones"
Origin Raised from a cross between "Frau Karl Druschki" and unnamed seedlings and introduced in 1958, centenary of the apparition at Lourdes. It was the first great success resulting from the happy meeting of George Delbard, head of a famous rose-growing firm, and André Chabert, an experienced rose breeder trained by his father and by Charles Mallerin.
Description Very few modern roses still command so much interest and admiration fully 30 years after their introduction as "Centenaire de Lourdes." It is a vigorous shrub which in suitable ground will grow to a height and width of almost 2 m. (6½ ft.). Its principal attraction is its numerous groups of double, cup-shaped flowers, consisting of 15 or so petals in a glowing satiny pink.
Use Groups of up to three plants; standard with trailing branches.

---

122 ICEBERG

Synonyms "Schneewittchen" (original name), "Fée des Neiges"
Origin A variety raised in 1958 by Reimer, son of Wilhelm Kordes, who since his youth had assisted his father in a series of carefully researched breeding programs. This rose was from "Robin Hood" (an early Hybrid Musk) x "Virgo" (a Mallerin-Meilland Hybrid Tea variety).
Description Very vigorous growth with large, shiny dark green leaves. Double, scented white flowers which may take on pink flushes in autumn. Extremely free flowering in clusters along the entire length of branches. Light pruning and fertile soil allow it to grow to shrub size. It can withstand even the coldest winters. If the site is poorly ventilated or planting too dense it may be attacked by mildew and black spot. "Iceberg is one of the WFRS-designated "World's Favorite Roses." In 1968 a reasonably vigorous and recurrent climbing variety was introduced, with other characteristics as in the original form.
Use Standard or shrub. Suitable for hedges and for group bedding; cut flowers.

123 GARDEN PARTY

Origin Herbert C. Swim, breeder for Armstrong Nurseries of Ontario, California, raised this variety in 1959 from "Charlotte Armstrong" x "Peace," two parents that have left their mark on many roses produced in the second half of this century.

Description A vigorous bush, 80–110 cm. (32–44 in.) high, with upright growth, plenty of basal shoots and well branched; persistent clear green leaves, reddish on reverse. The large buds open into big double flowers up to 12 cm. (5 in.) across, slightly perfumed, the petals creamy white with pinkish flushes that are particularly noticeable in autumn. Strongly recurrent. In 1960 "Garden Party" was one of the three roses chosen in the All-America Rose Selection, the other two varieties of that year being "Sarabande" and "Fire King," both raised by Francis Meilland in France. The previous year "Garden Party" had won the Bagatelle Gold Medal and the top Certificate of Merit in Madrid.

Use Groups of three or more plants.

124 TROPICANA

Synonym "Super Star" (United Kingdom)

Origin Mathias Tantau, 1960; according to the family tree that he drew up (cf. Jack Harkness, *The Makers of Heavenly Roses*), there were 40 crosses preparatory to the appearance of "Tropicana."

Description This was the first rose to exhibit a glowing vermilion coloring, and it was the major success story of its time. Growth is vigorous, maximum height 1 m. (3 ft.), upright, with few branches; the stems at first bear single flowers but there may be five or more on the same stem in autumn; flowering continues intermittently until the arrival of the frosts. Slightly fragrant. The climbing form is also well established. "Tropicana" won a dozen awards in Europe and the United States. In 1986, after 26 years in gardens, it gained 8.6 points out of 10 in the annual American Rose Society classification, having been included in the 1963 list and winning the Gold Certificate in 1967.

Use Cut flowers; small groups in flower bed.

125 PICCADILLY

Origin Sam McGredy raised this variety in 1959 when he was still based in Northern Ireland, before transferring his business to New Zealand. The cross between a yellow variety ("McGredy's Yellow") and a red ("Karl Herbst") produced a fine bicolored rose in which both yellow and red are prominent.

Description A bush about 70 cm. (28 in.) tall, compact but well branched; the branches are very thorny and the lovely glossy green foliage has coppery reflections. The stems often bear several flowers with some 15 bicolored petals (scarlet with golden-yellow base and reverse) which are especially brilliant when they first appear, but less so in summer heat or exposure to prolonged sunshine. In wet areas it may be subject to black spot. Twenty years after its introduction, "Piccadilly" was still one of the top 15 Hybrid Teas listed by the RNRS. It won the Royal Horticultural Society's Award of Merit and gold medals in the international trials at Rome and Madrid in 1960. It has produced a number of sports, including "Harry Wheatcroft" with yellow petals and prominent red striping.

Use For bedding, with plants set close together, 40–50 cm. (16–20 in.) apart.

---

126 PUREZZA

Origin In his attempts to breed unusual roses, Quinto Mansuino of San Remo, Italy took up, in the 1950s, the work begun by Attilio Ragionieri of Florence. From the miniature "Tom Thumb" x *R. banksiae lutescens* Mansuino obtained thousands of seeds which germinated successfully but failed to develop thereafter. Of a hundred or so surviving seedlings, one-third inherited the dwarf characteristics of *R. c. minima* (in the form of "Tom Thumb"), one-third the climbing attributes of *R. banksiae*, and the rest intermediate features. One variety which emerged from the second group showed exceptional qualities of strength and recurrence and was named "Purezza" for its white petals. In 1960 it won the Gold Medal at the Rome international trials in the novelty class.

Description A rambling rose, thornless and extremely vigorous. The small, glossy, elongated leaves are typical of *R. banksiae*. The very plentiful flowers are white, most of them double, of differing sizes—flat, very early-blooming, in clusters; some have long and narrow petals, others are bigger. The spring flowering is very prolific and prolonged; in temperate-warm zones there may be a modest recurrence in autumn and early winter.

Use After an initial period of getting established, it produces very long shoots which can be trained in umbrella or mushroom form.

127 ZAMBRA

Origin A variety raised by Meilland from crosses of two successive seedlings, both the result of the repeated cross "Goldilocks" x "Fashion" (1961). It won gold medals at the international trials that year at Rome and Bagatelle, and was described in some publications as "Rose of the Year." The "zambra" is a very energetic Spanish dance described as a "whirling flamenco," and the name is intended to show off the gleaming petal colors.
Description A rose with spreading growth, medium-sized, height about 50 cm. (20 in.), foliage glossy dark green. The trusses of five to eight flowers are far enough apart to show off the attractive shape and striking mixture of yellow and orange-red on the upper side of the petals, with yellow reverse. Recurrence is virtually continuous and the fragrance is fleeting. In some areas it is prone to attacks of black spot and mildew.
Use Patches of color for bedding; cut flowers.

128 ROYAL HIGHNESS

Synonym "Königliche Hoheit"
Origin "Virgo" and "Peace," both Meilland varieties, are the parents which gave delicacy and vigor to this variety, raised in 1962 at the Swim & Weeks nurseries in California.
Description A vigorous upright bush which can grow to a height of 1 m. (3 ft.), well branched, with glossy dark green leaves; large double flowers of exceptional beauty, light pink and of graceful shape, are borne singly on stout stems. The petals are slightly scented. Preventive treatment against disease is recommended as well as temporary protection against hard, prolonged frosts. Does not like rain. In 1960 it won the Gold Medal for new roses in the trials at Portland, Oregon, in 1962 the Gold Medal at Madrid, and in 1963 (along with "Tropicana") it was included in the All-America Rose Selection.
Use Bedding; cut flowers.

129 ISABEL DE ORTIZ

Origin Combines the qualities of the two varieties from which it was raised, "Peace" and "Kordes Perfecta." Reimer Kordes of Sparrieshoop, Federal Republic of Germany, raised and introduced it in 1962.

Description A vigorous rose, growing to 70–80 cm. (28–32 in.) with prolific healthy, glossy dark green foliage. Single-flowered stems, whose buds with pointed tips open into flowers 12 cm. (5 in.) across, beautifully shaped with 50 cherry-red petals, silver-white on the reverse, pleasantly perfumed for indoor arrangements. Does well in fairly dry climates and withstands harsh winter temperatures.

Use Grouped for bedding; standard; cut flowers.

130 FRAGRANT CLOUD

Synonyms "Duftwolke" (original name), "Nuage Parfumé" (France)

Origin Mathias Tantau, distinguished rose breeder from the Federal Republic of Germany, is rarely explicit in naming the parents of his excellent varieties. All he says about "Fragrant Cloud" is that it comes from an unknown seedling x "Prima Ballerina," another of his highly scented red roses. He introduced it in 1963.

Description The growth habit has sometimes been criticized, but the rose has many positive qualities: vigor, long stems, fine foliage and, above all, large, well-shaped flowers with 25–30 coral-red petals with a strong, penetrating scent. During the first flowering the stems bear single blooms but later, in the long recurrent period, anyone looking for single flowers is advised to remove supernumerary buds. This is the fourth variety to be described as "World's Favorite Rose" and it has won many other important awards, especially in the U.K. from the Royal National Rose Society and the Royal Horticultural Society.

Use The long stems, the shape of the flowers and their perfume make them ideal for cutting.

131 PAPA MEILLAND

Origin Meilland (France, 1963), from two of the most successful dark red roses, "Chrysler Imperial" x "Charles Mallerin." Both have velvety scarlet petals, probably inherited from their direct ancestors—"Tassin" and "Mirandy" respectively—and from their other antecedents.

Description It is fairly widely agreed that varieties such as "Charles Mallerin," "Josephine Bruce," the climber "Guinée" and other similar roses are the darkest tone of red, whereas the petals of "Papa Meilland" are a somewhat warmer dark crimson. Apart from their admirable color, the flowers, as might be expected in petals of this tone, are highly fragrant. The plant, reasonably vigorous, has an upright habit, growing to a height of about 70 cm. (28 in.), with glossy dark green foliage often prone to mildew. It is fairly free-flowering and recurrent.

Use The strong perfume and the elegant shape of the flowers make this variety an excellent florist's rose.

132 PASCALI

Origin Raised by Louis Lens (Belgium, 1963) from "Queen Elizabeth" x "White Butterfly." The name points to the association of the white of the petals with Easter (Ital. *pascale*).

Description Jack Harkness, who raised "Margaret Merill," today arguably the best of the white Cluster-Flowered varieties, used "Pascali" as the female parent. His opinion of "Pascali" is that this should be the choice of any gardener looking for only one white rose, since it gives excellent results in the garden and provides the most beautiful cut flowers. The vigorous bush grows to more than 1 m. (3 ft.); the foliage is a healthy, glossy dark green; the long stems bear excellently shaped flowers with some 25 petals—white, occasionally flushed cream, almost without scent—which are long-lasting even when cut. It was included in the All-America Rose Selection and is perhaps the only variety to have won an award in all the European trials for new roses. The current listing (1986) of the American Rose Society is 8.7 out of a total of 10.

Use Standard; mass of white in flower bed; cut flowers.

133 JOSEPH'S COAT

Origin An American variety raised in 1964 from "Buccaneer" x "Circus," all three bred by Herbert C. Swim for the Armstrong Nurseries of Ontario, California.

Description In places enjoying a mild climate, trained against a wall, this rose is a climber which can grow to 3 m. (10 ft.); otherwise it assumes a shrubby habit; it is covered with abundant dark green leaves which are not normally prone to fungal diseases. As the name suggests, the petals are multicolored, including milk-white, yellow, orange and red, deepest in autumn. There is a faint perfume. In 1964 this rose won the Gold Medal at the Bagatelle trials and two certificates of merit in Rome and from the National Rose Society (trial ground at St. Albans).

Use A shrub, given suitable support; in milder climates a moderately strong climber.

134 BLUE MOON

Synonyms "Mainzer Fastnacht" (original name), "Sissi"

Origin Introduced in 1964 by Tantau, Federal Republic of Germany, from unnamed seedling x "Sterling Silver" (double lilac scented flowers). When this variety made its first appearance in the splendid rose garden of the Tête d'Or park in Lyons, all the leading rose growers were present. They suggested to Mathias Tantau that his very beautiful new "blue" rose had an unpronounceable name in non-German-speaking countries and proposed calling it "Sissi." This was unacceptable in the United Kingdom because it was, with a different spelling, a common term for an effeminate person, and so it was named "Blue Moon."

Description After more than 20 years, most rose experts classify it as the best or at least among the best of the so-called blue roses. The shades of its silver-pink and lilac petals are very attractive, and the penetrating scent is an additional bonus in this lovely variety. The bush has an upright habit and is moderately vigorous, but the leaves are unremarkable.

Use It is seen to better advantage in a table arrangement than in the garden, preferably combined with a clear pink florist's variety such as "Sonia" or "Lara."

135 STARINA

Origin Raised in 1965 by Marie L. Meilland in France. It is a seedling from two vigorous shrub roses ("Dany Robin" x "Fire King") in turn crossed with "Perla de Monserrat," a Miniature variety with red flowers raised 20 years previously by the Spanish breeder Pedro Dot, one of the pioneers in the revival of such roses. This provides further confirmation of the dwarfing influence of Miniature varieties in crosses with bigger roses.

Description A vigorous bush with plenty of basal shoots, which in fertile ground grows to a height of 35 cm. (14 in.). Small glossy dark green leaves; well-proportioned double flowers with 25 petals, 4 cm. (2 in.) in diameter, beautifully formed; the slightly scented petals are a glowing blend of carmine, orange and scarlet. Continuously recurrent and resistant to all the most common diseases. In the international trials of 1968 at Tokyo and Rome "Starina" won top awards and its positive qualities have become increasingly apparent, as attested by the 1986 classification of the American Rose Society, which awarded it the exceptional score of 9.6 points out of 10.

Use Flower borders; tubs and window-boxes on balconies and patios.

136 TOURMALINE

Origin Raised by André Chabert of Georges Delbard S.A., this variety was named after the very hard mineral with light-polarizing properties, sometimes used for making jewelry, because its flowers seem positively luminous.

Description A bush well endowed with basal shoots, of medium size, growing to a maximum height of 80 cm. (32 in.), with sparse leaves and long single-flowered stems. The big double flowers, exquisitely scented, are notable for the unusual carmine-pink edging to the white petals which in some cases provides a delicate touch and in others spreads down on both sides. The rose is continuously and abundantly recurrent. In the spring and summer of 1965, the year it was introduced, "Tourmaline" received a series of important awards: the Gold Medal and title of "loveliest rose in France" at Lyons, the Gold Medal of the Société Nationale d'Horticulture de France, and the Gold Medal in the international trials at Madrid.

Use In rose beds designed to provide cut flowers for the house.

137   MARIA CALLAS

Synonym "Miss All-American Beauty"

Origin "Chrysler Imperial" x "Karl Herbst;" Marie L. Meilland, who raised the rose in 1965, did not avail herself of the enormous varietal choice of roses for breeding offered by Meilland but, according to *Modern Roses*, used one variety from the United States and another from the Federal Republic of Germany. It was named after the great American opera singer (of Greek origin); it is not known why the name was altered in the country of her birth.

Description The large flowers, 12 cm. (5 in.) and more across, with 50 scented petals, the vigor of the plant and the many healthy leaves that cover it from top to bottom are the qualities which brought the rose enormous success in the United States; more than 20 years after its introduction, the All-America Rose Selection awarded it 8.5 points out of 10.

Use One or more bushes in the flower bed; medium-height dividing hedge.

---

138   VERSAILLES

Synonym "Castel" (in countries not allowing geographical names)

Origin Raised in 1967 by André Chabert, breeder for the French firm of Georges Delbard. Parentage: ("Queen Elizabeth" x "Provence") x ("Michèle Meilland" x "Bayadère.")

Description This rose may have determined a change in the taste of enthusiasts who, having previously shown an overwhelming preference for varieties in shades of red, were seduced by the soft mother-of-pearl pink coloration of "Versailles." The new trend was confirmed by the ten awards, including four gold medals, which the variety received in 1967. The strong, sturdy bush, growing 1 m. (3 ft.) high, has glossy foliage, firm stems and a fleeting perfume.

Use Grouped in flower beds; grown separately for cut flowers.

139 FRED LOADS

Origin R.A. Holmes of Stockport, England, raised this variety in 1967 from "Dorothy Wheatcroft" x "Orange Sensation."

Description Janet Browne, present publications editor of the Royal National Rose Society, described this variety in *The Rose* as "vigorous and spectacular." It is indeed a sturdy plant, growing to more than 2 m. (6½ ft.), its upright habit being reminiscent of "Queen Elizabeth;" and the single or semi-double scented flowers, about 10 cm. (4 in.) across, produced in large clusters, are a striking soft orange-vermilion. The leaves are large, glossy, light green. The rose is exceptionally free-flowering and recurrent. In 1967 the RNRS awarded "Fred Loads" its Gold Medal and the Royal Horticultural Society its Award of Merit. In the early years following its introduction, it took second or third place in the RNRS classification of the 24 best shrub roses, and since 1977 it has held first place uninterruptedly.

Use As background color to the rose bed; hedging.

140 PHARAOH

Synonym "Pharaon"

Origin From ("Happiness" x "Independence") x "Suspense" (Meilland, 1967).

Description Even today this is a much esteemed rose, with long-lasting, very big, well-shaped velvety scarlet double flowers. The bush is vigorous, 80 cm (32 in.) tall, and the foliage is healthy. These attributes won it gold medals in international trials at Geneva, The Hague and Madrid, and the title "loveliest rose in France" in 1967. The awards are all the more significant because—contrary to expectations of a rose with dark red, velvety petals—"Pharaoh" has no fragrance.

Use Massed group of this variety.

141 NOZOMI

Origin A naturalist and amateur rose breeder who later turned professional, Toru (Susumu) Onodera of Urawa, Japan, raised "Nozomi" in 1968 from a Climbing Miniature variety, Ralph Moore's "Fairy Princess," and the Miniature bush "Sweet Fairy," raised by Jan De Vink in 1946. The name "Nozomi" means "hope" in Japanese.

Description The sturdy yet flexible shoots can climb to more than 1.5 m. (5 ft.) if attached to a trellis, or can be used to trail over the ground. The tiny, glossy leaves are a perfect accompaniment to the small, single, flat flowers, pale pearl in color, which are slightly scented and bloom in abundant trusses throughout the single, long summer flowering period. It is best to grow non-grafted specimens.

Use A climber, given adequate support; ground cover; trailer.

142 ANNE MARIE TRECHSLIN

Synonym "Anne Marie"

Origin Assuming that rose breeders had the freedom of choice enjoyed by painters in selecting any color they wanted from the palette, one might say that in order to produce this rose Mme Louisette Meilland took the soft yellow of "Peace," the gold and apricot of "Sutter's Gold," the rich red of "Demain" and the individual tones of other antecedents such as "Mme P.S. du Pont" (golden-yellow) and "Dr. Kirk" (yellow, nasturtium and coral). The combination of skill, chromosomes and luck enabled her on this occasion to raise a quite remarkable rose.

Description A vigorous bush of upright growth, smooth branches with stout but well-distanced thorns and leaves which, when young, are mahogany-red like the long stems, and when adult large, dark green and persistent. The long, pointed buds open into well-shaped flowers, multicolored (coral, pink, orange and yellow), with a powerful citrus fragrance. Color and scent may vary in different climates and surroundings. Although the flowers age rapidly, the compensation is their abundance and recurrence. In the Monza international trials of 1968 the rose was awarded the Gold Medal for the most highly perfumed variety.

Use Bedding.

143 BARONNE EDMOND DE ROTHSCHILD

Origin Raised by Louisette Meilland and introduced in autumn 1968. This is one of the loveliest of many splendid roses produced for Meilland by this most experienced breeder. Parentage: ("Baccara" x "Crimson King") x "Peace."

Description A sturdy bush growing about 75 cm. (30 in.) high, similar in habit to "Peace." Its arrangement of 40 petals (ruby-red with silvery reverse) is not unlike that of "Isabel de Ortiz." The deep scent, the sturdiness of the plant and its ease of growth were contributing factors to its winning the title of "loveliest rose in France" in 1968, the Gold Medal in the international trials in Rome, and the replica of the crown of Queen Theodolinda for the most fragrant variety at the Monza trials. From 1974 it has also been available in its climbing form, and this has all the bush's attributes as well as additional vigor.

Use Grouped for bedding; standard.

144 SUNBLEST

Synonym "Landora"

Origin As with other varieties from Mathias Tantau, we have little information about the background of "Landora" (1970) except that the final cross was between an unnamed seedling and "King's Ransom," that splendid, vigorous American rose with yellow flowers.

Description A sturdy rose of rapid growth and notable resistance to low temperatures, with an open habit and large, healthy light green leaves. The big but slender bud opens its 35 petals gradually to produce a slightly scented bright canary-yellow flower.

Use Representative rose bed; section for cut flowers.

145 LILY DE GERLACHE

Origin The Experimental Station for Ornamental Plants of Melle, Belgium raised this variety from a cross between Wilhelm Kordes's "Perfecta" and Mathias Tantau's "Prima Ballerina," and it was not to be supplied to enthusiasts if the results were not first-class. After rigorous tests from 1969 to 1971 at the Royal National Rose Society's trial grounds, "Lily de Gerlache" emerged with a trial ground certificate and the award of the Edland Memorial Medal for the most highly scented rose. Other awards were given at the trials in Courtrai, Belgium, and The Hague, Holland. The variety was finally marketed in 1971. It was named after the Baroness de Gerlache de Goméry, founder and at that time president of the Société Royale Nationale Des Amis de la Rose (Belgium) and past president of the World Federation of Rose Societies.

Description A bush of upright habit with healthy, tough, dark green leaves. The large pointed buds open into highly fragrant flowers with 50 petals, a mixture of pink and red, borne on stems either singly or in clusters. The plant is free-flowering and recurrent, with excellent resistance to cold and to disease.

Use Bedding, with a recommended distance of 35 cm. (14 in.) between plants; cut flowers.

146 GRAND NORD

Origin Chabert-Delbard raised this variety, which was introduced in 1973 and is still one of the "stars" in the Georges Delbard catalog of 1985–6 in the section entitled *Les roses qui font les beaux bouquets*.

Description A very vigorous shrub which in fertile soil will grow to a height of 1.2 m. (4 ft.); the long upright stems sometimes bear single flowers but more often one flower already opened and three or four tight buds. The 26 large petals are white and are sometimes flushed ivory or cream, not changing but heightening the basic color. It is sturdy and very free-flowering.

Use The upright habit encourages its additional use as a dividing hedge or to flank either side of a path.

147 YESTERDAY

Synonym "Tapis d'Orient"

Origin The breeder of this "modern rose which has the charm of old roses" was Jack Harkness, who raised it from ("Phyllis Bide" x "Shepherd's Delight") x "Ballerina," introducing it in 1974.

Description This vigorous Polyantha is a small, dense bush which grows to 1 m. (3 ft.) or a little more, profusely covered with thick clusters of small flowers made up of a dozen scented petals in shades of pink culminating in a touch of lavender. Recurrence is more or less continuous. "Yesterday" has won gold medals in the trials at Bagatelle and Baden Baden, the Royal National Rose Society's Certificate of Merit and the Royal Horticultural Society's Award of Merit.

Use Single specimens or groups; small free hedge; elegant indoor arrangements.

148 DOUBLE DELIGHT

Origin The cross between two successful American varieties ("Granada" x "Garden Party") produced "Double Delight" in 1976. The name may be taken to apply both to the double charm of the rose's color and scent and to the ever-varying patterns of red and white on the petals.

Description The rose begins to grow vigorously after the year needed to become established, and this probably led to some unfavorable initial criticisms. But the variety's steady improvement is attested by the American *Proof of the Pudding* feature in the American Rose Annual, assessing new roses; the American Rose Society awarded "Double Delight" 8 points out of 10 in 1977, 8.5 out of 10 in 1979 and 9 out of 10 in 1986. In a suitable climate and soil the plant is vigorous, with handsome foliage and a growth habit midway between upright and open. The large flowers, with about 40 petals, measure more than 12 cm. (5 in.) across, but the principal attributes are the original color and the penetrating perfume. Awards include gold medals in the trials at Rome and Saverne in 1976 and the cup for perfume at Geneva in the same year. It was also one of the three winners in the 1977 All-America Rose Selection.

Use Bedding; cut flowers.

149 MARGARET MERRIL

Origin A variety raised by Jack Harkness of Hitchin, England, in 1977 from ("Rudolph Timm" x "Dedication") x "Pascali."
Description A bush of moderate height with plenty of vigor, well branched, with upright habit. Its flowers have uncommon attributes: the elegant shape of the corolla (25–30 petals) which would make this Floribunda in the bud the envy of any Hybrid Tea; the ivory color with a powder-pink flush in some of the centers; and the penetrating scent, which has so far not been equaled by any variety in this class. Awards include gold medals in international trials between 1978 and 1982 in Rome, Geneva, and New Zealand; prizes for the most highly scented rose in Geneva, St Albans (RNRS), Monza, The Hague and New Zealand.
Use Representative rose beds.

150 LA SEVILLANA

Origin This variety paved the way for a series of bush and shrub roses of varying height, Cluster-Flowered, with balanced growth and considerable decorative effect, to which the Sélection-Meilland has devoted particular interest from 1977 to the present day. The name, following a pattern set by other Meilland varieties with bright colors, refers to a celebrated Spanish dance.
Description A vigorous rose with regular growth, uniform, with plenty of basal shoots; dense foliage initially bronze-green, then dark green, highly disease-resistant. Flowers with 12–15 petals, extremely bright and luminous, at first orange-red, then scarlet, their clusters festooning the plant from base to tip, blooming in greater or lesser measure from late spring to late autumn. It also withstands frosts. In 1980 it won the Gold Medal at the international trials in Orléans for varieties already on the market.
Use Patches of color (with three plants to the square meter); dividing hedge.

151 SILVER JUBILEE

Origin Here we must go back to 1952 and *R. kordesii*, which came about through spontaneous chromosome doubling and was used by Wilhelm Kordes to produce many good varieties. Subsequently the Scottish breeder Alec Cocker crossed one of these varieties, "Parkdirektor Riggers," with "Piccadilly" and then the resultant seedlings with Hybrid Teas, and after eight years of experiments produced "Silver Jubilee." This masterpiece was introduced in 1978, but unfortunately Cocker had died at the end of the previous year. The name commemorated the 25th anniversary of Queen Elizabeth II's accession to the throne.
Description The rose is considered the prototype of a new generation with vigorous growth and plenty of basal shoots, regularly and compactly branched; the dense, glossy foliage is resistant to disease and almost extends to the flower stalk. The main attraction is the beautifully shaped corolla with petals that open slowly, new blooms appearing continuously for as long as faded flowers are removed. The color is pink with a red flush, and the intensity of the scent depends on atmospheric conditions. In 1977 the Royal National Rose Society awarded "Silver Jubilee" the President's International Trophy, given for the year's best variety, and a Gold Medal. For six years it has occupied first place among the Hybrid Teas in the RNRS annual classification.
Use Bedding; cut flowers.

152 SWANY

Origin Ten years ago Meilland concluded its experimental research into new types of roses (Meidiland and Meillandécor) designed to meet a number of different requirements: decorative effect, vigor, ease of maintenance, absence of wild pollen (propagation occurs through cuttings) and marked resistance to disease and intense cold. These varieties were intended in the main for parks and large public areas but also for specialized private use, such as ground cover and for trailing purposes; "Swany," a rambler, fulfills this latter function. Similar roses have been raised by other European breeders such as Kordes, Lens, Poulsen and Interplant, and the prospects are good for an increasingly large and widespread supply for professional rose growers, garden architects and park departments.
Description and use After initially growing upright, the branches tend to spread along the ground or trail over a wall. "Swany," with its characteristic flexible branches, has white double flowers in rosettes, blooming for a considerable time and with slight recurrence, especially in a sunny climate. Three shrubs should be planted to the square meter.

153   SNOW CARPET

Origin Sam McGredy, director of McGredy Roses International, represents the fourth generation of his family and is also the fourth to bear that particular forename. The hundred-year-old business operated from Portadown, Northern Ireland, until 1972 when it transferred all activities to Auckland, New Zealand, where climatic conditions were more favorable. The fourth Sam McGredy was responsible for opening new vistas with his Miniature ground-cover roses and his now famous "hand-painted roses," and is continuously on the lookout for novelties. The parents of "Snow Carpet" are a Miniature and a climbing Miniature ("New Penny" x "Temple Bells"), their immediate antecedent being the vigorous *R. wichuraiana*, a rambler and ground-cover rose whose branches extend to more than 6 m. (20 ft.).

Description A variety raised in 1978 and introduced in 1980. It is beautifully proportioned with minute leaves, long and slender trailing branches and miniature flowers with 40 tiny white petals; in spring these cover the plant in its "snow carpet." It won the Gold Medal in the international trials at Rome in 1981.

Use Broad patch of white amid surrounding lawn; trailer from high-positioned bed.

154   REGENSBERG

Synonym "Buffalo Bill" (France)

Origin This variety, raised in 1979 by Sam McGredy, belongs to the new class of "hand-painted roses." It forms a shrub with spreading growth and stems bearing clusters of large semi-double flowers; the petal color is red but in varying shades ranging from plum to violet-red; these tones merge or provide a kind of fringe to the inner part, which is white or cream. "Picasso," introduced by McGredy in 1971, was among the first of these roses, representing the fifth generation of a complex series of crosses that began with "Frühlingsmorgen," a shrub from Wilhelm Kordes, as well as *R. macrophylla coryana* and "Tantau's Triumph." Gradually the desired attributes were perfected and there were unforeseen variations in the color pattern; the series continued with "Old Master" (1974), "Matangi" (1974), "Eye Paint" (1975), "Priscilla Burton" (1978) and "Regensberg" (1979), but is certainly not complete, for these delightful and decorative color combinations appeared in 1981 in "Maestro," the first "hand-painted" Hybrid Tea.

Use Groups of three to five plants separated by other roses.

155 MARÉCHAL LECLERC

Synonym "Touch of Class" (in the United States, produced by Armstrong Nurseries)

Origin Despite 40 years of rose-growing experience and numerous gold medals, Michel Kriloff of Antibes, France, is a model of modesty and reliability. The scrupulous tests to which he subjected this variety is further proof of his thoroughness. It flowered for the first time in 1969 but was not marketed in France until the autumn-winter of 1979–80, after repeated confirmation of its lasting qualities. In 1984 the variety was subjected to cultivation tests in various testing grounds under the control of the American Rose Society, and in 1986 it won the All-America Rose Selection. The raiser has not provided much information about its background, simply indicating "Micaela" x unnamed seedling, both raised by Kriloff.

Description The bush is of upright growth, up to 1.5 m. (5 ft.) high; the healthy foliage is glossy dark green, and the elegant turbinate buds are followed by very large flowers with 25 salmon-pink to coral petals, shading to yellow at the base. Thanks to their consistency, the petals open slowly.

Use Typical garden variety.

156 PRISTINE

Origin This variety was raised in 1978 by W.A. Warriner for the American firm Jackson & Perkins Co. and was exhibited in various European trials in 1979–80. It won the Henry Edland Medal at St. Albans (RNRS) for the most highly perfumed variety, the Gold Medal at Rome and the Silver Medal at Monza. In the United States the 1986 classification of exhibition varieties placed it first with 1,169 votes; and in the selection from all garden varieties it received the top vote with 8.9 out of 10.

Description A very decorative bush even when not in flower, with large dark green leaves, fairly upright habit and single-flowered stems. The annual of the American Rose Society defined both its major virtue and its major defect in pointing out that it was not the most free-flowering of roses but that it certainly produced the loveliest flowers. The long buds open to reveal 25 ivory-colored petals with the faintest flush of pink and a fleeting perfume; flowering is prolific early but trails off thereafter.

Use In groups in the rose bed and in section for cut flowers; it is best to pick them when the buds are barely open.

157　ANNA FORD

Origin The characteristics of this variety emphasize the free-flowering tendencies of small-sized roses and the dominant trait of miniaturism in crosses between these and bigger roses. The parents of "Anna Ford" are "Southampton," an extremely vigorous bush rose growing to a height of 1.2 m. (4 ft.), and "Darling Flame," a Miniature from Meilland. It was introduced in Britain in 1980 and was named after the very popular television newscaster.

Description A small but vigorous bush, height 20–25 cm. (8–10 in.), with trusses of brilliant, well-shaped, semi-double flowers, deep orange in color, tending to become paler before the flower fades but maintaining the yellow at the base. After the flowers fall, the hips have a small crown of silvery sepals at the tip, making the rose look like the Swiss edelweiss. The stems are straight, very thorny, with toothed leaves. It can withstand the coldest winter conditions.

Use Edges of rose bed; small hedge.

158　LAS VEGAS

Origin A Hybrid Tea ("Charlotte Armstrong" x "Mission Bells") introduced in 1981 by its raiser, Reimer Kordes, who had collaborated with his father as a rose breeder since 1955.

Description A bush with dense, branching growth, up to about 80 cm. (32 in.) high, notable for its floriferousness and recurrence. The 1986 Kordes catalog called it the most beautiful Hybrid Tea, bicolored in shades of orange. The bud is long and pointed, the flowers, elegantly shaped, are moderately double, a bright, clear orange above and yellow with flushes of red on the reverse. Its recurrence and its number of flowers bring "Las Vegas" into the Floribunda class: its drawback is the short duration of the blooms at their best. This variety won the Gold Medal at Geneva in October 1985 in the recurrent roses category.

Use Bedding.

159 PRINCESSE DE MONACO

Origin In 1956 the late Francis Meilland introduced "Grace de Monaco," a variety raised from a cross of two of his loveliest roses, "Peace" x "Michèle Meilland." Three hundred bushes were planted in a special bed in the gardens of Her Serene Highness but after 25 years some had died, others were dying and no replacements could be had. In June 1981 Princess Grace attended sessions of the jury at the Salon de la Rose, which that year was being held in Monte Carlo, and voiced her admiration for a rose with 30 large petals, their purple-red borders merging with the creamy white ground underneath (the flag of Monaco has two horizontal bands, one red, the other white).

Description The rose, reaching a height of about 75 cm. (30 in.), is regular in growth and fairly upright; the tough leaves are a shiny dark green. The stems almost always carry single flowers; it is consistently recurrent; the flowers are fleetingly fragrant.

Use Bedding and cut flowers.

160 BONICA '82

Origin This Meilland bush rose, introduced in 1982, reused the name given toward the end of the 1950s to another Meilland variety in the Hybrid Polyantha class. The reasons were the lack of suitable alternative names, the high costs of patenting and the high qualities of the original rose.

Description A compact bush, growing to 60–80 cm. (24–32 in.), with plenty of vigor; open growth with dense, relatively small dark green foliage. Each stem bears 5–10 flowers with 25–30 petals initially bright pink, then paler—almost double, abundant during the only long flowering period. The variety is highly resistant to disease and intense cold.

Use A rose that is particularly suitable for mass planting in areas with cold climates. It is best to plant three shrubs to the square meter.

161 MOUNTBATTEN

Origin Some years ago the Soldiers', Sailors' and Airmen's Families Association requested R. Harkness & Co. to name a new rose after the organization. Since neither the full name nor the initials (SSAFA) were really suitable, an alternative was sought. Because the late Lord Louis Mountbatten had been president of the association for 25 years and Jack Harkness had served with him in Burma during World War II, it was unanimously decided to call the rose "Mountbatten." The complex breeding program had begun in 1973, and among the varieties in the pedigree of the new rose were "Peer Gynt," "Anne Cocker" and "Southampton." In 1979 it won the Royal National Rose Society's Certificate of Merit. On May 12, 1981 the rose was chosen as part of the wedding bouquet of Lady Diana Spencer, subsequently Princess of Wales. In 1982 it was designated "rose of the year" for the United Kingdom and in that same year it won gold medals in trials at Orléans and Belfast.

Description Shrubby growth and upright habit, height about 1.5 m. (5 ft.), glossy foliage, stems with a few flowers which can be reduced to one by disbudding; rounded corollas have some 45 mimosa-yellow petals; slight scent. The variety is highly resistant to cold.

Use Single specimens; hedges, cut flowers.

162 CÉLINE DELBARD

Origin The collaboration between André Chabert and Georges Delbard has proved enormously successful and this variety, raised by the firm in 1983 from two unnamed seedlings, was named by Georges Delbard after his second granddaughter.

Description A bush of open habit, growing to a medium height of 60–70 cm. (24–28 in.), with dense foliage resistant to mildew. The cone-shaped buds open into semi-double, cup-shaped flowers with 15–20 petals, which can measure up to 10 cm. (4 in.) across, in clusters on individual stems and with a faint scent. The petals glow in two colors, soft salmon-pink above and a delicate pinkish-white on the reverse. The plant is literally covered, in the course of the first flowering period, in flowers which continue to appear later, also in fair numbers. It received the Gold Medal for Cluster-Flowered roses in the 1983 trials at Monza.

Use Uniform group; a lovely choice for those fond of pastel shades.

163 YVES PIAGET

Origin Meilland, who raised this spectacular variety and introduced it in autumn 1984, have not provided information as to its pedigree, but there is good reason to suppose that one of its antecedents was that great nineteenth-century rose "Paul Neyron," recognizable even in the petal color.

Description A very vigorous bush, growing to 80–90 cm. (32–36 in.), its habit intermediate between upright and spreading; healthy, fairly inconspicuous foliage. The most important feature of this variety is undoubtedly the flowering habit (continuous and generally with single blooms), the very large, almost globular corollas measuring about 13 cm. (5 in.) in diameter, with some 80 scented petals; the flowers, when open, look as much like peonies as roses. In the international trials at Geneva in 1982 "Yves Piaget" set records, winning the three most important awards: the Gold Medal diploma with an award from the city, the cup for the most highly perfumed variety and the gold rose for the variety with the most points. It received another cup for perfume at the Bagatelle trials and further gold medals in Tokyo and Monza.

Use Bedding: cut flowers.

---

164 MODERN ART

Origin The Danish firm of Poulsen takes the credit for introducing the first roses raised from crosses between Polyanthas and Hybrid Teas, so producing the class of Hybrid Polyanthas, including the pioneer varieties such as "Rödhatte" (1912), "Else Poulsen" (1924), "Kirsten Poulsen" (1924) and "Anne Mette Poulsen" (1934), which have brought so much beauty to gardens everywhere. Although the parents of "Modern Art" are not officially listed in rose publications, this did not prevent it gaining the Gold Medal (with most votes) for new roses at the trials in Rome (1984).

Description A bush with regular growth, 60–70 cm. (24–28 in.) high, with large, tough dark green leaves and stems carrying flowers either singly or in clusters; in both cases the blooms are large and well-shaped, with 25–30 petals measuring some 12 cm. (5 in.) across. The color is velvety orange, deeper along the edges, creamy-yellow on the reverse. It is very free-flowering and recurrent, with an agreeable perfume.

Use Bedding.

Synonym "Viorita" (outside the U.K.)

Origin The series of crosses made by Jack Harkness that ultimately produced this variety include "Blue Moon," "Lilac Charm," "Orange Sensation," "Allgold" and *R. californica*. It was introduced in the autumn-winter of 1984–5 and won both the Gold Medal for the best in its category (Cluster-Flowered roses) and the gold rose for the highest number of points at the international trials in Geneva. It also won the Gold Medal at Monza.

Description This is a modern version of the small-sized Poly-antha but stronger in constitution—resistant to cold, with a spreading growth habit; the luxuriant foliage is pale green. The semi-double flowers have 20 violet-red petals, more or less cup-shaped with a decorative tuft of golden-yellow stamens in the center; there are 5–10 flowers to each cluster. The scent can be noticed only when atmospheric conditions are right. In the U.K. proceeds from the sale of this rose have largely gone to charitable organizations.

Use Edges of rose bed; small groups.

166 ARTISTE

Origin The breeding program was carried out at the Roseraies Dorieux of Montagny, France; the parents were "Playboy," a Cocker (1976) variety with fiery red flowers, and "Zambra" (Meilland, 1961), with glowing yellow and orange corollas. It won silver medals at Bagatelle and Rome and gold medals at Courtrai and Geneva, having been introduced in autumn 1984.

Description The authorities responsible for the rose garden of a large European city where this variety is featured declared that it flowered every single day from spring to autumn. It is a vigorous bush, about 70 cm. (28 in.) high, with medium-small, deep green, glossy wavy-edged leaves. The clusters of 10–20 large, single flowers grow from the tips of sturdy upright stems; the color is light pink with bright red margins, the reverse pinkish-white, turning pale as the flower fades.

Use Bedding.

167 LOUIS DE FUNÈS

Origin For some years it has been the frequent custom of Meilland not to provide information as to the parentage of their new roses. The variety "Louis de Funès," introduced in autumn-winter 1984–5, is no exception to this rule. The actor de Funès was a keen gardener and rose enthusiast who, when filming on the Côte d'Azur, was invited to visit the Meilland experimental grounds where their unnamed roses are grown after passing numerous tests. Louis de Funès expressed particular interest in one particularly glowing bicolored rose, and this was named after him on the spot.

Description A bush of upright habit, strong branches and medium height, about 1 m. (3 ft.). Shown off to great effect against the lovely glossy foliage are the huge double flowers with more than 30 petals, measuring 14 cm. (6 in.) in diameter, bicolored in tangerine with a pale yellow reverse and remaining at their best for some time. The stems start by bearing single flowers but gradually come to carry several blooms.

Use Typical bedding rose; can be grown as a standard.

168 BORDURE VIVE

Origin The parentage of this variety, marketed in the 1985–6 season, is given as unnamed rose x ("La Fayette" x "Walko"). "Joseph Guy" (="La Fayette") was a low-growing Polyantha dating from 1921; "Walko," raised in 1957, was one of the first successes of the Delbard-Chabert collaboration; and the un-named rose in the formula was crossed with a seedling born of this union, so producing "Bordure Vive." The variety is a colorful addition to the series initiated by "Bordure Rose"—about 50 cm. (20 in.)—and "Bordure Jaune," 40 cm. (16 in.).

Description This is regarded as the smallest of the Cluster-Flowered roses, about 30 cm. (12 in.) in height. Each cluster bears 4–8 corollas formed of some 24 petals, cyclamen-pink with a cream center and a uniformly clear pink reverse. It flowers very early and abundantly; the blooms are long-lasting and recurrence is virtually continuous. Preventive treatment against diseases is recommended in areas where black spot is preva-lent. "Bordure Vive" won a gold medal in Madrid in 1984 and a silver medal at Monza in the same year.

Use Massed color; edges of rose bed; rock garden; tubs and window-boxes.

169 LAVENDER DREAM

Origin The Dutch firm Interplant has rapidly gained an international reputation. In the trials at Rome in 1984 this interesting variety won the Gold Medal for Cluster-Flowered roses and, in the same year, the Royal National Rose Society's trial ground certificate. In late May 1986 it won the three most important awards at Monza: the Queen Theodolinda crown for the most highly perfumed variety, the Gold Medal for Cluster-Flowered roses and the "City of Milan" cup for the variety best suited to growing in public gardens. Its parentage is "Yesterday" x "Nastarana" (the latter probably an unmarketed variety from Interplant). The presence of "Yesterday" in the genetic makeup of "Lavender Dream" is evident; the variety is likely to combine well with other classic garden roses.

Description A vigorous rose with a habit that is initially erect, so as to form a compact bush, and then tends to spread with ground-covering attributes. The prolifically flowering clusters consist of tightly packed blooms, each 4–5 cm. (2 in.), semi-double and scented, their color pink, lilac and white; in full flower they entirely conceal the small-medium dark green leaves. The plant is reliably recurrent.

Use Good color contrast to surrounding lawn; suitable for borders of embankments and large rock gardens.

---

170 MME DELBARD

Origin This is the rose that adorned the cover of the 1985–6 Delbard catalog, and it celebrated two coincidental happy occasions: the golden wedding of M. and Mme Georges Delbard and the 50th anniversary of the business he opened on 9 November 1935 at 16 Quai de la Mégisserie in Paris. The antecedents of "Mme Delbard" include, among others, "Super Star," "Samourai," "Gloria di Roma," an unnamed variety from Meilland, another from Tantau and "Impeccable," a veteran (1955) from Delbard-Chabert.

Description It is rare for a rose distinctive for its cut flowers when grown under glass to enjoy so much success outdoors in the garden, but before it was commercially introduced "Mme Delbard" won a gold medal for varieties grown under glass and other awards for roses cultivated out of doors at Tokyo, Coutrai, Le Roeulx and Saverne. The rose is healthy and vigorous, with plenty of basal shoots and an upright habit; the abundant foliage is dark green; the stems almost always bear a single flower, large with 35 or more petals, the glowing, velvety red being maintained until the flower fades. Each bloom opens slowly, the petal edges curving slightly outward as if to highlight the slender central part.

Use Bedding; cut flowers either under glass or outdoors.

171 SOURIRE D'ORCHIDÉE

Origin It is always considered risky to attribute the characteristics of a new variety to a particular ancestor, and it is virtually impossible to do this in the case of "Sourire d'Orchidée;" only one of its parents is known, "Age Tendre," a Hybrid Tea with beautiful pink double flowers raised 20 years previously by Paul Croix at the Bourg-Argental nurseries at Lyons, France, a firm soon entering its second century of existence. "Sourire d'Orchidée" was first offered for sale in the autumn-winter of 1985–6, having previously won important awards at Rome, Baden Baden and The Hague and two top prizes (Gold Medal and golden rose) at Geneva.

Description A climbing rose with vigorous growth, up to 3 m. (10 ft.) or more in height, and lovely, healthy foliage. The spring flowering envelops the plant in dense, translucent, mother-of-pearl clusters which persist, though in lesser numbers, until the autumn

Use Trained fan-wide against a wall or trellis.

172 PIERRE DE RONSARD

Synonym "Eden Rose"

Origin ("Danse de Sylphe" x "Händel") x "Kalinka," raised by Meilland. One wonders what distant ancestor was responsible for the old-fashioned grace of the spherical flower with its tight arrangement of milky-white petals, flushed with pink that is deeper around the margins. Its immediate parents, especially "Kalinka" and "Händel," contributed their flower color; but the particular charm of the rose surely goes further back in time, for it seems to be born of the imagination of a great artist from Sèvres or Capodimonte. Distribution is to begin in the autumn of 1986 in Germany, where the name "Eden Rose" will be adopted; in 1987 it will be available in France and other countries under its original name.

Description A climbing rose of moderate growth; the larger flowers blend well with the big, abundantly produced leaves; their uncommon beauty is revealed when the buds open into opulent double flowers, which continue through spring and summer; there is slight perfume; the plant is resistant to disease.

Use Can be grown with a fairly upright habit against a fence or trellis.

Origin It has already been mentioned elsewhere that as a result of the intervention (for reasons unknown) of natural factors, radiation or chemical products introduced artificially, the bud of a shrub may produce a branch with characteristics different from those of the original plant. The mutation of a shrub rose into a climbing rose (statistically the most common) has recently occurred in "Orange Meillandina," one of the first of the Meilland Miniature roses, raised at Antibes, France, to produce a climbing sport in 1986.

Description "Cl. Orange Meillandina" is vigorous in growth, considering the dwarf nature of the variety, reaching a height of 1.5 m. (5 ft.). The leaves retain more or less the appearance of the original (tightly packed, small, bright green leaves); each truss bears 1–3 relatively large flowers, measuring almost 5 cm. (2 in.) across; about 50 brilliant vermilion petals tend at first to be shaped like a cup and gradually flatten out; there is practically no perfume. Raised in the 1980s, the first of the "Meillandina" roses quickly formed a family; this variety had small dark green leaves and proportionately sized double red flowers, but subsequent varieties exhibited a wide range of other shades (white, yellow, yellow-orange, pink, scarlet, and red streaked with white); among these "Orange Meillandina" stood out for its depth and persistence of color, its freedom of flowering and its recurrence, comparable to a geranium but with the advantages of longer duration, resistance to cold and compact growth.

Rose lovers are now offered the climbing sport of "Orange Meillandina." One point to remember is that even though the plant is some four times taller than the original, this does not mean four times as many flowers, although the overall number is obviously greater. This is true of all mutations of shrub to climbing roses. One thing seems guaranteed—a promising future for Miniature roses.

Use In small gardens and for adorning low fences and walls; ideal for growing in window-boxes and other containers on patios, terraces and balconies.

174 BLAZE

Origin The parentage ("Paul's Scarlet Climber" x "Gruss an Teplitz") announced in 1932 by the raiser has been debated and contested even in old editions of *Modern Roses*, where the raiser's name was followed by a list of all his varieties. Beside "Blaze," a variety attributed to Joseph W. Kallay of Painesville, Ohio, was the note: "Origin disputed." In fact, whereas numerous affinities with "Paul's Scarlet Climber" have been recognized, these are less evident in the case of "Gruss an Teplitz," leading some to claim that the presence of the latter variety in the pedigree is simply due to the fame which this "parent of proved reliability" acquired in the early 1900s.

Description Climber with clusters of large flowers; recurrent (1932). "Blaze" is a vigorous climber with semi-double scarlet flowers, lightly scented. Horace McFarland writes in *Roses of the World in Color*, "The rose 'Blaze' came into existence in an advertizing blaze that started up like a rocket and almost came down like its stick. Deemed to be a recurrent blooming form of 'Paul's Scarlet Climber,' it was and is just that. After it has been established in the ground, and as it later came to be propagated from blooming wood, it does recur and do justice to its name." In 1950 the firm of Jackson & Perkins marketed an "improved Blaze." From spring to autumn the overall number of flowers produced by "Blaze" and "Paul's Scarlet Climber" is about the same, but the latter gives its best show in late spring and early summer. The *Handbook for Selecting Roses* gives "Blaze" 7.8 points out of 10, and "Paul's Scarlet Climber" 7.7 out of 10.

Use Pergolas.

175 ECLIPSE

Origin Jean Henri Nicolas, who raised this variety, was born around 1880 at Roubaix in northern France. The young Frenchman obtained a degree in Natural Sciences, took out American citizenship and brought a professional approach to what had hitherto been an amateur attitude to rose growing when he joined the important firm of Jackson & Perkins, gaining a reputation here as a breeder and eventually becoming its Director of Research. Nicolas related (in *A Rose Odyssey*) that there was a story attached to the name "Eclipse," for on August 22, 1932—the day the first seedling flowered—there was a memorable eclipse of the sun.

Description Rose with large recurrent flowers (1932). The elegant, tapered bud of this variety marked a turning point in the evolving design of hybrid roses. In the 1950s it was still being grown under glass for florists. The color and fragrance of the petals, the long stem, the consistent, glossy foliage and the vigor of the shrub all helped to earn "Eclipse" gold medals in international trials at Rome, Portland and Bagatelle, and to win the American Rose Society's David Furstenberg Prize. In 1986 "Eclipse" was awarded 6 points out of 10 by the American Rose Society.

Use Bedding; cut flowers.

176 BETTY PRIOR

Origin Raised from "Kirsten Poulsen" (or more probably, given its similarity, from "Else Poulsen"); the other parent is unknown. Hybrid from Priors Nurseries, Colchester, England.

Description During the first thirty years of the present century, the name of Polyantha rose was applied to any low-growing variety used for creating large patches of single color in the garden. Around the middle of the last century, the Poulsen family emerged as the leading rose growers in Denmark; Dines, one of the founder's sons, conducted experiments by crossing Polyanthas with Hybrid Teas. Two varieties thus produced appeared to possess remarkable qualities and were named respectively "Else Poulsen" and "Kirsten Poulsen," both notable for large clusters of five-petaled flowers, exceptional vigor and a height of over 50 cm. (20 in.). Their offspring retained these characteristics and were responsible for the creation of a new class (Hybrid Polyanthas), of which "Betty Prior" is an excellent representative. It is free-flowering (particularly in autumn) and the bright crimson of its five handsome petals blends delightfully with the young foliage and mahogany-red branches.

Use As dividing hedges, in groups or as single specimens.

177 MISTER LINCOLN

Origin "Charles Mallerin" and "Chrysler Imperial" were the two "black" roses (separately described) used for cross-breeding by the Californian rose-growing firm of Swim & Weeks to produce this variety. It proved its worth over several years and was given the prestigious name of "Mister Lincoln;" in 1964 it was introduced commercially by Conard Pile of West Grove, Penn.

Description Bush rose with large recurrent flowers (1964). The defects and merits of both parents have been mentioned under their respective headings, and expectations of greater freedom of flowering and recurrence were justified in the case of their offspring; furthermore, the flowers satisfied the most rigorous tests for color, perfume and consistency. The slender buds open slowly to reveal 30–40 velvety, deep red petals, the corollas measuring almost 15 cm. (6 in.) across. The cut flowers, kept under suitable conditions, remain fresh for several days. The shrub, upright in habit, grows to a height of 80 cm. (32 in.), the flower stems being long and stiff, the foliage dark green. In 1965 it was one of the two winners in the All-America Rose Selection; the 1986 *Handbook for Selecting Roses*, issued by the ARS, awarded "Mister Lincoln" an exceptional 9.1 points out of 10.

Use For representative display in the garden; also for cut flowers.

GLOSSARY

Anther   the male sex organ on the tip of the stamen.

Bicolor   a rose with petals in a different color on each side.

Budding   propagating a rose by grafting a leaf-axle bud into the neck of a rootstock.

Budding union   the point at which the bud is inserted and from which the new shoots grow.

Calyx   the collective term for the five sepals.

Carpel   the style, stigma and ovary; collectively the female parts of the flower.

Dead-heading   the removal of dead blooms and hips to increase recurrence.

Die-back   fungus attack causing shoots to turn brown.

Eye   or leaf-axil bud. The bud from which a new shoot will grow.

Genus   a group of plants of one or more species which have common botanical characteristics.

Heeling in   planting a rose temporarily if proper planting cannot be done at once.

Hip   (or hep) the seed pod of the rose.

Hybridizing   creating a new rose by cross-fertilization – the transfer of pollen from one to another.

Maiden   a rose in its first season after budding.

Moss   the resin-coated glands on a Moss rose.

Mutation   a genetic change in a plant which can produce a sport.

Pedicel   the flower stem or footstalk.

pH scale   the measurement of soil acidity. 7.0 on the scale means the soil is well balanced. Around 6.8 or slightly acid is ideal for roses.

Reversion   a hybrid reverting to the characteristics of one or other parent.

Rootstock   the roots of a wild rose onto which a cultivated variety is budded to give it added vigor and other desirable characteristics.

Rose sick   a term describing soil in which roses have been grown for some years and in which new roses will not grow well. Cause uncertain.

Sepals   the five triangular components of the calyx which protect the unopened flower.

Species   plants that have distinct and unique botanical characteristics and breed true from seed. A division of a genus.

Sport   produced by a mutation when a flower or shoot on a plant differs in size or color from that of the other flowers or shoots.

Sucker   a shoot growing from the rootstock.

Variety   a naturally occurring variation on a species. One produced in cultivation is a cultivar, though the term variety is often used for both.

INDEX

Picture Sources

With the exception of pp. 62–3, 70–1 and entries 23, 64, 73, 77, 94, 131, 161, which were kindly provided by Mr R.C. Balfour, all the photographs in this book are from Stelvio Coggiatti's private collection.